y matter as you may think for; However, let me see; there's,
Harry & Sarah & Dick & Eliza & Septimas & Peter
arles & Betsey & Harriet & Reb mma & Bob &
n' Mothers & Father & Mother & ther & Mother &
Carry & Cousin Amelia & Cou Uncle Edward &
two housemaids,
me if I can
use.
John dear
forget the tw

PEOPLE COUNT

A history of the General Register Office

OFFICE OF POPULATION CENSUSES AND SURVEYS

PEOPLE COUNT

A history of the General Register Office

Muriel Nissel

LONDON: HER MAJESTY'S STATIONERY OFFICE

FRONT COVER
Detail from *Marriage by Registrar,* an
engraving by W B Boucher based on a
painting by W Dendy Sadler. An
artist's watercolour impression
prepared especially for this book.

END-PAPERS
The Census troubles of a large family
(George Cruikshank)

Contents

Foreword

This is the history of an Office which has for 150 years provided two important services for the people of England and Wales.

First, working with Local Authorities, it has organised the civil registration of births and deaths, and also civil marriage. Muriel Nissel's book is a tribute to the way in which the Registration Service has carried out these tasks. Registration Officers throughout the country seek to conduct the marriage ceremony in a way that makes it an important individual occasion, not just an official proceeding. They also take professional pride in helping people to provide accurate information, often at an emotional time. These records are important to the individuals themselves for legal and other purposes, and they provide a gold mine of information for people wanting to discover their family origins. The Public Search Room in London is often packed with people in pursuit of legal documentation or historical records.

But from the very start, my predecessors saw a second value in the records: the provision of good quality statistics about the population. This book records the gradual development of this function, with the Office taking over the running of the Census, and more recently the NHS Central Register and the processing of statistics about hospital patients, and merging with the Government Social Survey. It also records the growing use of the statistics derived from these sources, from William Farr's early work on cholera and other 19th century health hazards to a multitude of uses for policy analysis and management in both the public and private sectors today.

Throughout all the changes, the original approach to registration has remained remarkably stable and that is the greatest possible tribute to those, especially Thomas Lister and George Graham, who originally established the service. Today, demands for information and services increase apace, and modern technology opens up endless new possibilities. Our aim must be to meet these challenges with equal success.

Mrs G.T. Banks
Registrar General

Acknowledgements

I would like to thank the many people who have helped in the preparation of this book. It had to be written in a very short space of time and without their ready co-operation and speedy return of drafts it would not have been possible. It would be invidious ever to try to list the large number of individuals within OPCS but I wish to single out the Press Officer, Sheenagh Wallace, who at all times gave imaginative and quiet support. Of those outside OPCS, I owe a particular debt to Professor E Grebenik, Professor AM Adelstein and Dr D Eversley; also to Mr David Usherwood who nobly lent me his wordprocessor when mine broke down, and to Her Majesty's Stationery Office who gave their valuable help and advice, particularly in the design of the publication.

In producing this book I have collaborated with various people in OPCS, but I should like to stress that the views expressed are mine and not necessarily shared by OPCS.

MURIEL NISSEL

May 1987

The author wishes to thank the following for permission to reproduce illustrations and extracts:

British Journal of Sociology, pp 64–5

British Library, pp 11, 16 (bottom left), 17, 58

Public Records Office, pp 3 (top), 8 (bottom), 9 (top right, bottom right) 10, 54, 76, 87

Telegraph and Argus, Bradford, pp 15 (top), 26

Cartoon reproduced by permission of *Punch* magazine, p 62

The Trustees of the British Museum, p 8 (top) and endpapers

Wellcome Institute Library, London, p 115

Keighley Register Office, p 12

Edward Arnold (publishers) Ltd., pp 50, 125, 126

Registration before 1837

Today

Today some 260 million records of births, deaths and marriages in England and Wales are stored in St Catherines House in the Aldwych in London, the headquarters of the General Register Office, or the Office of Population Censuses and Surveys as it is now called. The Public Search Room, where the eight and a half thousand volumes of indexes of these records are kept, has some half a million visitors each year. Until 1973 the records themselves were kept in nearby Somerset House, a beautiful eighteenth century building originally designed to house, in the words of Anthony Trollope, 'a nest of public offices': these included the revenue departments, known as the Salt, Stamp, Excise, Land Tax, Hawkers and Pedlars, Hackney Coaches and Lottery Offices, as well as a number of other offices such as those concerned with the administration of the Crown Lands and the Navy and the Office of Sick and Wounded Seamen. A number of distinguished royal societies also moved into Somerset House and the Royal Academy held its first exhibition there in the spring of 1780. In 1837 the Royal Academy moved into a new building in Trafalgar

An eighteenth century engraving of Somerset House, the premises of the General Register Office from 1837 to 1973

Square, the present National Gallery, and the rooms it vacated were allocated to an important new office, the General Register Office.

St Catherines House is a much more prosaic affair and the search room itself is much like any other store room, with iron racks stretching as far as the eye can see filled with heavy leather-bound volumes containing indexes of births, marriages and deaths dating from 1837 when the Office was first established. The birth indexes are bound in red, marriages in green and deaths in black. They were held in quarterly volumes until 1984 when they were replaced by annual volumes. Some of the early ones (of 'hatches, matches and dispatches' as they are sometimes irreverently called) still contain the original entries in a fine flowing script, reminiscent of the kind of copy book exercises which faced children of earlier generations in their first days at school. In 1871 the Registrar General suggested that these early indexes should be printed to guard against loss and to make it easier for the public to refer to them. They would also take up much less space. Every year the public 'were applying more numerously for certificates' and the change would better enable the Office 'to meet the demands upon the search-room staff'. His proposal was not adopted. However, from 1866 to 1910 the indexes were printed; from 1910 to 1970 they were typed and from then on they have been printed by computer.

The search room is usually thronged with people. On average there are some two thousand each day, with more in the school holidays. What are they doing there? What are they looking for? They fall into two main groups. The first, accounting for some three quarters of all the visitors, are there out of curiosity, searching for their roots and the history of their families. They want to know where they come from, what kind of jobs their

An old lady from Blackburn visits the Public Search Room

I know that I'm the youngest of 16 and I know 8 of them but the other 8 I don't know when they were born – I know their names vaguely but I was just coming to see if I could find their full names in the register and how they came in the family – which order they came in.

My father worked in the Townhall at Blackburn and my mother, up to being married was a weaver then she didn't work after she was married. But the kindest mother anyone could ever wish for – never got out of patience with any of us though she had 16 she was never out of patience – she was the kindest mother anybody could ever wish for so . . . I was going to look through the register but I thought they would all come in a family but they don't – I've got to look individually so that means I've got to look at all the books individually.

My grandfather was a valet but I never knew any of my grandparents so they couldn't help me so I've got to look out for myself.

The Public Search Room: Somerset House in the nineteenth century (above) and St Catherines House (below)

ancestors had, whether something unexpectedly interesting might turn up. One old lady, the youngest of sixteen children, had known only eight of them and she had come to see if she could trace the remaining eight. She knew that they had all been born in Blackburn and she vaguely recalled their names, so she was hoping to find out in what order they were born and what their full names were. Many visitors come from overseas and many groups include children helping in the quest. They tend to cluster round the earlier indexes dating from 1837, when the system began, until the end of the nineteenth century. When they come in they are advised how to set about tracing records and the leaflet on 'family trees' warns that finding out about ancestors may involve a series of searches:

Notes for visitors to the Public Search Room.

> If a person wishes to trace the record of his father's birth but does not know when he was born it may be necessary first to search for the record of the father's marriage . . . . A certificate of the marriage should give the bridegroom's age and the name of his father, and so will give a starting point for tracing and identifying the record of the birth concerned. A certificate of that birth will give the names of the parents, including the mother's maiden name, and the process may be repeated for the preceding generation.

The second group, who crowd round the later volumes, have a much more immediate and practical purpose in mind. They need copies of birth, marriage and death certificates for all kinds of legal and administrative purposes. About half the applications to St Catherines House are for copies of birth certificates, about 30 per cent for marriage and 20 per cent for death certificates. Today these documents are essential for establishing eligibility for a wide range of welfare payments from child benefit to funeral costs, for passports, schooling, settlement of estates, insurance payments and so forth. One of the searchers, thumbing through the 1966 January–March births index, said that she wanted a certificate because she urgently needed a new passport: she had left her previous one behind at her parents' home in Newcastle and they were unable to find it for her. Applying for a passport is one of the more frequent reasons for obtaining copies of birth records. Standing next to her was a young man who had been asked for his birth certificate by a prospective employer: he thought he had given it to his previous employer who had never returned it. A young Australian was searching for evidence of her grandfather's birth certificate to support her right to stay in the United Kingdom. At the back of the search room, where the marriage indexes are kept, a woman was searching the April–June index to enable her to get a copy of her marriage certificate so that she could start divorce proceedings. Some of the visitors were professional searchers,

Early leather-bound volumes of birth indexes in the Public Search Room. The entries are the original, written in a flowing, handwritten script.

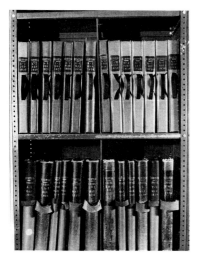

An extract from a 1912 marriage index, the first year when the surname of the second party was shown in the index alongside the surname of the other party.

particularly probate searchers employed by firms of solicitors and executors to trace relatives of people who had died. This can sometimes be very difficult, particularly if Christian names and surnames are common ones, because the evidence has to stand up to scrutiny in a court and leave no room for doubt.

The actual records are not open to the public, only the indexes which provide the necessary details for obtaining copies. The original registers of births, deaths and marriages are held locally in the districts where the events were notified and if copies are subsequently needed, they can be obtained from the local registrar. A copy of each register entry, however, is sent to OPCS headquarters where it is microfilmed and a duplicate set is thus held centrally. It is from this source that the searchers at St Catherines House obtain their copies: over a quarter of a million are issued annually. Anyone applying in person – and on average over a thousand a day do so – can obtain a full certificate of birth, marriage or death for a fee of £5. An application by post costs £10.

Yesterday

This is the situation today, 150 years after civil registration began. How would our searchers have fared if they had needed to establish their rights through birth, death or marriage before 1837?

The main records were the parochial registers of baptisms, burials and marriages instituted by an injunction in 1538 of Thomas Cromwell, Henry VIII's Lord Chancellor, instructing the clergy of every parish to keep registers of all the baptisms, weddings and funerals at which they officiated. It was an ecclesiastical system with no statutory authority; baptisms, for example, though serving as evidence of age, parentage or succession to property, were essentially a by-product of the religious rite of baptism. The injunction was repeated, and penalties for neglect prescribed, by an Act in 1597 in the reign of Queen Elizabeth I. This, for the first time, directed that transcripts of the registers should be sent annually to a diocesan registrar. The purpose was much the same as it is for the civil registers of today – the protection of the original record against alteration by providing a copy with which it might be compared in case of dispute or loss by fire or decay.

Although this obligation to supply copies to the diocesan registry was often ignored, the bringing together of the registers in one place for a large area meant that they could more easily be arranged and consulted. In 1590, Lord Burghley, Lord Treasurer to Queen Elizabeth, perceived how these records of christenings, weddings and burials might be brought together nationally to provide statistics both for England and Wales as a whole and also for each county:

Lord Burghley, Lord Treasurer to Queen Elizabeth I, in 1590 foresaw the need for a national register.
(*Report from the Select Committee on Parochial Registration, 1833*)

that there should be yearly delivered a summary of the whole whereby it should appear how many christenings, weddings and burials were every year within England and Wales and every county particularly by itself, and how many men-children and women-children were born in all of them, severally set down by themselves.

Producing national statistics however was no business of the Church, nor could it easily be fitted into its administrative framework.

The Act of 1597 was implemented with varying degrees of success and in the middle of the next century the government seriously considered taking registration out of the hands of the clergy. Many registers were far from complete and others had been lost by fire or flood and even eaten by rats. Frequently transcripts were not sent to the diocesan registrar. Failure to record events in sufficient detail meant that it was often difficult to identify the person to whom they related and carelessness over the security of the records made it easy to forge or falsify the entries. All this made litigation more complicated: in particular, if it was not possible to obtain proof of pedigree or even of legitimacy then the right of inheritance was difficult to establish.

During the seventeenth and eighteenth centuries an important factor affecting the completeness of the registers was the growing number of people who supported Nonconformist religions instead of the Established Church. Although registers were kept by the Jews and the Quakers and many of the Free Churches and Chapels, they were outside the Established system and were thus unacceptable as a source of national records or of vital statistics. Furthermore they were not in law entitled to be treated as of the same validity as the parochial registers. This was understandably resented by Nonconformists and contributed to the steadily growing conviction that the parochial system was no longer able to meet national requirements. Moreover, there was a growing interest in the question of whether the country's population was increasing or diminishing, and it was clear that records of baptisms and burials could not be as reliable for studying these changes as records of births and deaths which would form the basis of a civil registration system.

Of particular concern during the eighteenth century was the increasingly unsatisfactory state of the marriage law. During the time of the Commonwealth (1652–1660) a law, which came into effect in 1653, provided for civil marriage similar in many respects to that of today. Twenty-one days notice had to be given to a registrar elected for each parish and published by being 'cried in the market place' or by fixing a notice in some public place. A certificate of the performance of the publication, containing the particulars of the parties and signed by the registrar, was authority for the marriage to proceed. It might then be celebrated, in the presence of at least two witnesses, by a Justice of the Peace, recorder, alderman, sheriff or town clerk. The registrar received one shilling for taking and publishing the notice and issuing his authority (certificate) and another shilling for registering the marriage.

One of the marriages celebrated in the chapel of the Fleet Prison in the eighteenth century. The verse at the foot of the engraving reads:

Between a brisk young Sailor & his Landlady's Daughter at Rederiff.

*Scarce had the Coach discharg'd its trusty Fare
But gaping Crouds surround th'amorous Pair;
The busy Flyers make a mighty Stir!
And whisp'ring cry, d'ye want the Parson, Sir?*

*Pray step this way — just to the Pen in Hand
The Doctor's ready there at your Command:
This way (another cries) Sir I declare
The true and ancient Register is Here:*

*Th'alarmed Parsons quickly hear the Din!
And haste with soothing Words t'invite 'em in:
In this Confusion jostled to and fro,
Th'inamour'd Couple know not where to go;*

*Till slow advancing from the Coache's Side,
Th'experienc'd Matron came (an artful Guide)
She led the way without regarding either,
And the first Parson spliced 'em both together.*

The illustrations below and on pages 9–10 show entries made by one of the 'Fleet Parsons', Ashwell, in his register at the time of performing the marriage ceremony.

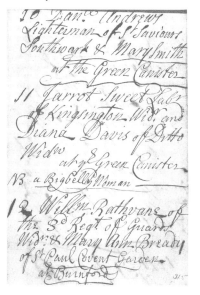

On the restoration of the monarchy in 1660 all Acts of the Commonwealth became void and marriage registration reverted to its previous state. Not only were the registers themselves inadequate and incomplete but there was often insufficient preliminary enquiry by the clergy. Attempts by the Government to prevent secret matrimony in churches led to serious abuses in other directions. The most notorious was in the City of London, which claimed exemption from ecclesiastical jurisdiction, and where a widespread traffic sprang up catering for furtive marriages from all over the country. One such register relates to the Fleet Prison which records marriages celebrated in the prison chapel by, so it is surmised, a number of clergyman imprisoned there for debt. Many marriages were not solemnised in any place of worship at all and a great number actually took place at taverns. Marriages were good for business and innkeepers vied amongst each other to attract eloping couples. The Mint register in Southwark for 1733–1736, for example, is not just a register of marriages but also a fascinating source of information about the low taverns and brandy shops in that neighbourhood and of the somewhat exotic signs under which they were known. Thus one is described as 'Mrs. Silver's Brandy Shop, the Harrow and Dunghill'. Ashwell, one of the 'Fleet parsons', includes in his registers odd notes and comments which throw light upon the many disreputable features underlying the formal marriage entry. He describes his clients as 'rude people', 'very abusive people', 'most notoriously vile behav'd' and so on. One entry, on 27th August 1743, records 'Peter Fly of St. John's Clerkenwell and Ann Sharp. N.B. after the sd. marriage of Fly it appeared he was a Rogue and had a Wife alive.' Some of the marriages, however, were in rather a different class. The Duke of Hamilton used the secrecy of the system to marry Miss Gunning, and Henry Fox, father of Charles James Fox, married a daughter of the Duke of Richmond[1]. Quite possibly, too, a number of wealthy young men may have woken up one morning after a night in town to find themselves married to ladies whom they would, on consideration, perhaps rather not have married.

Despite strong opposition in the House of Commons, including that of Henry Fox, the Government set about tightening up the law with a Marriage Act, known as Lord Hardwicke's Act, which came into force in March 1754. Before that date, the decision as to who could marry and how, was a church prerogative. The new Act now drew the State into the legal distinction between marriage and cohabitation and the structure of family law which stems from it. The Act stringently enforced the preliminaries to marriage and required the consent of parents or guardian for the marriage of a minor. It laid down that marriages (unless by special licence) must take place during specified hours in the parish church in the presence of at least two witnesses and in all cases by a clergyman of the Church of England. The marriage had to be registered at once in the parish marriage register (the form of which was prescribed), and only certificates from these were to be admissible as evidence of marriage. Exceptions were made for Jews and Quakers as an acknowledgement of the scrupulous manner in which those communities were accustomed to publicise, celebrate

The practice of solemnizing clandestine marriages, so prejudicial to the peace of families, and so often productive of misery to the parties themselves thus united, was an evil that prevailed to such a degree as claimed the attention of the legislature. The sons and daughters of great and opulent families, before they had acquired knowledge and experience, or attained to the years of discretion, were every day seduced in their affections, and inveigled into matches big with infamy and ruin; and these were greatly facilitated by the opportunities that occurred of being united instantaneously by the ceremony of marriage, in the first transport of passion, before the destined victim had time to cool or deliberate on the subject. For this pernicious purpose, there was a band of profligate miscreants, the refuse of the clergy, dead to every sentiment of virtue, abandoned to all sense of decency and decorum, for the most part prisoners for debt or delinquency, and indeed the very outcasts of human society, who hovered about the verge of the Fleet Prison to intercept customers, plying like porters for employment, and performed the ceremony of marriage without license or question, in cellars, garrets, or alehouses, to the scandal of religion, and the disgrace of that order which they professed. The ease with which this ecclesiastical sanction was obtained and the vicious disposition of those wretches open to the practices of fraud and corruption, were productive of polygamy, indigence, conjugal infidelity, prostitution, and every curse that could embitter the married state.

Smollett describes the Fleet marriages at the time of Lord Hardwicke's Act in 1754.
(*Eighth Report of the Registrar General 1845*)

Establishing the General Register Office

Opposite, the public notice announcing the new system of birth and death registration – June 1836. Under the direction of the Registrar General the Board of Guardians were required to fix such notices on the outside of churches or chapels, and other conspicuous public buildings or places.

Organisation of the registration service

One of the major issues which had to be settled before civil registration could be established was what local arrangements were practicable. Should the clergy act as civil officers? Should the registrar be an elected officer, perhaps acting under the direction of the clergyman? Or should the appointment be entirely civil, and, if so, what should constitute a registration district and who should appoint the registrar?

Before the reform of local government setting up county councils in 1888, no suitable local authority areas existed. However, under the Poor Law Reform Act of 1834, Poor Law Commissioners were appointed for aggregates of parishes – called Unions – to administer poor relief and it was these 'Unions' which the 1836 Registration Act specified should form the basis of superintendent registrars' districts, the districts being further subdivided into registrars' districts for births and deaths registration. The Act further specified that the clerk to the Board of Guardians of each Union should, if he had the qualifications which the Registrar General considered necessary, also become the superintendent registrar. The subdivision of the area into districts

Registrars were required to inform the public of the penalties for supplying false information. This 1837 notice was displayed in the sub-district of Haworth, Yorkshire where the deaths of some of the Brontë family were recorded.

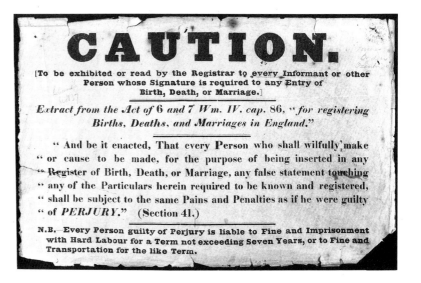

CAUTION.

[To be exhibited or read by the Registrar to every Informant or other Person whose Signature is required to any Entry of Birth, Death, or Marriage.]

Extract from the Act of 6 and 7 Wm. IV. cap. 86, "for registering Births, Deaths, and Marriages in England."

" And be it enacted, That every Person who shall wilfully make " or cause to be made, for the purpose of being inserted in any " Register of Birth, Death, or Marriage, any false statement touching " any of the Particulars herein required to be known and registered, " shall be subject to the same Pains and Penalties as if he were guilty " of *PERJURY*." (Section 41.)

N.B. Every Person guilty of Perjury is liable to Fine and Imprisonment with Hard Labour for a Term not exceeding Seven Years, or to Fine and Transportation for the like Term.

A letter to *The Times*, on 18 March 1837, objecting to the appointment of the Home Secretary's brother-in-law as the first Registrar General.

7, Dover-street, Piccadilly, March 14

Sir,—I enclose you the accompanying correspondence for your perusal and insertion in your paper, should you think the circumstances of sufficient importance.

The facts are briefly these:— In the year 1833 I was professionally concerned in a suit in which many hundreds of pounds had been fruitlessly expended in searching for baptisms, burials, &c., to make out a pedigree, and the plan of a general metropolitan registry became so apparent to my mind that I immediately set about a plan, the details of which I forwarded to Lord Brougham, then Lord Chancellor, and it was afterwards brought into the Commons by his lordship's brother, as you will see by the copy of my letter enclosed.

When I found that in the last session of Parliament the measure was about being triumphantly carried according to my original plan, under the protection of Lord John Russell, I considered myself fairly entitled, as the inventor or originator of the measure, (and especially it being one which will eventually prove a very considerable addition to the revenue) to the consideration of Government for an appointment in its direction and accordingly I wrote to Lord John Russell . . .

Immediately the bill had passed, I received a letter from his lordship's secretary . . . stating that his lordship had no appointment in his gift, and referring me to the parties authorized by the bill, but there I had no chance of success, having hitherto managed to live in my parish without the acquirement of popularity, or mixing myself up with parochial broils.

Notwithstanding the last answer, on the very next day I had the surprise of reading the appointment of T. H. Lister, Esq., (Lord John Russell's relative) as "Registrar General of Births, &c. in England and Wales," the very post to which I had aspired, to which I conceived myself entitled as the originator of the measure, and to the duties of which my experience in the matter, and being many years a member of the legal profession, rendered me fully competent.

This, Sir, clearly shows how patronage tyrannizes over right, and perhaps it may, through the medium of your journal, be hereafter explained, when, on the 15th of August last Lord John Russell stated he had no appointment in his gift, how it happened on the very following day his relative, Mr. Lister, was ushered into office? It might also be interesting to know, by whose patronage Mr. Lister obtained the appointment, and what were the nature of his claims or qualification for it. I have the honour to be, Sir,

Your very obedient servant,

A. F. EDWARDS

General in September 1836 by William IV whose letter patent for the appointment is reproduced as a colour plate. On 1 July 1837, the two Acts came into force, eleven days after the young Queen Victoria came to the throne. The new service was established and, at the same time, the General Register Office was founded in fulfilment of the need perceived with such vision by Lord Burghley nearly 250 years earlier.

References

1. Louis Kronenberger. *Kings and Desperate Men.* 1942, London, Gollancz.

Establishing the General Register Office

Opposite, the public notice announcing the new system of birth and death registration – June 1836. Under the direction of the Registrar General the Board of Guardians were required to fix such notices on the outside of churches or chapels, and other conspicuous public buildings or places.

Organisation of the registration service

One of the major issues which had to be settled before civil registration could be established was what local arrangements were practicable. Should the clergy act as civil officers? Should the registrar be an elected officer, perhaps acting under the direction of the clergyman? Or should the appointment be entirely civil, and, if so, what should constitute a registration district and who should appoint the registrar?

Before the reform of local government setting up county councils in 1888, no suitable local authority areas existed. However, under the Poor Law Reform Act of 1834, Poor Law Commissioners were appointed for aggregates of parishes – called Unions – to administer poor relief and it was these 'Unions' which the 1836 Registration Act specified should form the basis of superintendent registrars' districts, the districts being further subdivided into registrars' districts for births and deaths registration. The Act further specified that the clerk to the Board of Guardians of each Union should, if he had the qualifications which the Registrar General considered necessary, also become the superintendent registrar. The subdivision of the area into districts

Registrars were required to inform the public of the penalties for supplying false information. This 1837 notice was displayed in the sub-district of Haworth, Yorkshire where the deaths of some of the Brontë family were recorded.

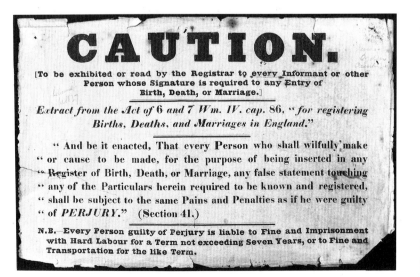

CAUTION.

[To be exhibited or read by the Registrar to every Informant or other Person whose Signature is required to any Entry of Birth, Death, or Marriage.]

Extract from the Act of 6 and 7 Wm. IV. cap. 86, "for registering Births, Deaths, and Marriages in England."

" And be it enacted, That every Person who shall wilfully make " or cause to be made, for the purpose of being inserted in any " Register of Birth, Death, or Marriage, any false statement touching " any of the Particulars herein required to be known and registered, " shall be subject to the same Pains and Penalties as if he were guilty " of *PERJURY*." (Section 41.)

N.B. Every Person guilty of Perjury is liable to Fine and Imprisonment with Hard Labour for a Term not exceeding Seven Years, or to Fine and Transportation for the like Term.

of Hamilton used the secrecy of the system to marry Miss Gunning, and Henry Fox, father of Charles James Fox, married a daughter of the Duke of Richmond[1]. Quite possibly, too, a number of wealthy young men may have woken up one morning after a night in town to find themselves married to ladies whom they would, on consideration, perhaps rather not have married.

Despite strong opposition in the House of Commons, including that of Henry Fox, the Government set about tightening up the law with a Marriage Act, known as Lord Hardwicke's Act, which came into force in March 1754. Before that date, the decision as to who could marry and how, was a church prerogative. The new Act now drew the State into the legal distinction between marriage and cohabitation and the structure of family law which stems from it. The Act stringently enforced the preliminaries to marriage and required the consent of parents or guardian for the marriage of a minor. It laid down that marriages (unless by special licence) must take place during specified hours in the parish church in the presence of at least two witnesses and in all cases by a clergyman of the Church of England. The marriage had to be registered at once in the parish marriage register (the form of which was prescribed), and only certificates from these were to be admissible as evidence of marriage. Exceptions were made for Jews and Quakers as an acknowledgement of the scrupulous manner in which those communities were accustomed to publicise, celebrate

The practice of solemnizing clandestine marriages, so prejudicial to the peace of families, and so often productive of misery to the parties themselves thus united, was an evil that prevailed to such a degree as claimed the attention of the legislature. The sons and daughters of great and opulent families, before they had acquired knowledge and experience, or attained to the years of discretion, were every day seduced in their affections, and inveigled into matches big with infamy and ruin; and these were greatly facilitated by the opportunities that occurred of being united instantaneously by the ceremony of marriage, in the first transport of passion, before the destined victim had time to cool or deliberate on the subject. For this pernicious purpose, there was a band of profligate miscreants, the refuse of the clergy, dead to every sentiment of virtue, abandoned to all sense of decency and decorum, for the most part prisoners for debt or delinquency, and indeed the very outcasts of human society, who hovered about the verge of the Fleet Prison to intercept customers, plying like porters for employment, and performed the ceremony of marriage without license or question, in cellars, garrets, or alehouses, to the scandal of religion, and the disgrace of that order which they professed. The ease with which this ecclesiastical sanction was obtained and the vicious disposition of those wretches open to the practices of fraud and corruption, were productive of polygamy, indigence, conjugal infidelity, prostitution, and every curse that could embitter the married state.

Smollett describes the Fleet marriages at the time of Lord Hardwicke's Act in 1754.
(*Eighth Report of the Registrar General 1845*)

and register their marriages. However, Dissenters and Roman Catholics were deprived of the possibility of marrying legally according to their own rites and, if they wished to establish evidence of the fact of their marriages, and hence the legitimacy and right of inheritance of their children, they had to accept the service of the Established Church. The new law, in contrast to the previous over-lax situation, thus appeared to many as excessively rigid and added to the growing pressure at the end of the eighteenth century for national civil registration of births, deaths and marriages.

An attempt had been made in 1753 to introduce more complete registration. Mr Potter put forward a Bill in the House of Commons for comprehensive and compulsory registration of births and deaths by the minister of the local parish 'whether the parent or person be of the Church of England or not'. The entries were to be made in special register books with printed headings for appropriate columns and copies were to be given to the local Overseer of the Poor. The Bill, however, also contained proposals for carrying out a census of population which attracted fierce opposition and led to the defeat of the Bill in the House of Lords.

Following the constitutional reforms of 1832 which widened the franchise and redistributed parliamentary seats, the House of Commons lost no time in appointing a Select Committee to inquire into the whole system of parochial registration. The Committee's conclusion was that there should be national civil registration of births, marriages and deaths, administered from a General National Office, and the two Bills which were subsequently introduced became the Registration Act and the Marriage Act of 1836. The Marriage Bill as originally drafted provided for a system of State preliminaries to marriage in the form of a Notice and Certificate by a registrar: this system was to be applied compulsorily to all marriages, Church or otherwise, and the banns system was to be abolished. Legal validity was to be accorded to the religious marriage ceremonies of any religious denomination, and civil marriage in a local register office was to be established for those who regarded marriage as a purely civil contract. Parish clergy were left to perform the registration of church marriages and the new registrars were to register all others. Marriage registration, like birth and death registration, was to be linked with the central supervisory authority.

In this form the Bill left the Commons, but the Lords made substantial changes. In particular the banns system was restored as an optional substitute for the State preliminaries. As soon as the Act was passed, Thomas Henry Lister was appointed Registrar

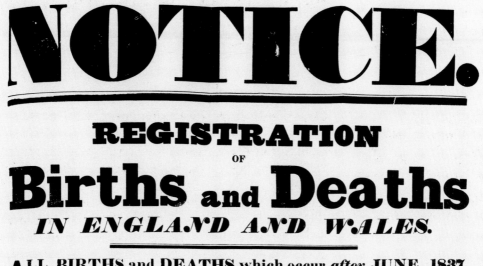

NOTICE.

REGISTRATION

OF

Births and Deaths

IN ENGLAND AND WALES.

ALL BIRTHS and **DEATHS** which occur *after* **JUNE, 1837,** may be registered by the Registrar of the District within which they occur, *without any Payment being required* from the Persons applying to have them registered, provided that, in the case of a *Birth*, it is registered within Six Weeks after the day of the Birth.

A BIRTH *cannot* be registered more than *Six Weeks after* the day of the Birth, without payment of **7s. 6d.**; nor can it be registered *at all* more than *Six Months* after the day of the Birth.

All Persons, therefore, should have the Births of their Children registered *without delay.*

The time at which a **DEATH,** happening after June, 1837, may be registered, is *not limited ;* but it is very desirable that it should always be done *as soon as possible.*

The **REGISTRAR** may be compelled to register a *Birth* or *Death*, if notice is given him of the *Birth* within Six Weeks after it, and of the *Death* within Five Days after it, by persons duly authorized.

Notice may be given to the Registrar either by word or by writing.

All Persons may give Notice; and it is to be desired that whosoever has an opportunity should do so.

The *Name* and *Dwelling-house* of the **REGISTRAR** of each District may be seen in a *List* which the Superintendent Registrar is required to publish.

Any person applying to have a Birth or Death registered will be told by the Registrar what kind of information is required.

No Birth or Death which occurs *before* **JULY, 1837,** can be registered.

General Register Office,
      June, 1837.

By Authority.—J HARTNELL, Printer, Wine Office Court.

was to be determined by the Board of Guardians, subject once again to the approval of the Registrar General.

From the date of his appointment in September 1836, the Registrar General set to work with astonishing speed and vigour. In his first annual report to the Home Secretary, Lord John Russell, he describes how he addressed a series of circular letters to all the Boards of Guardians pointing out the general principles which should determine the formation of districts and setting out the qualifications needed for both superintendent registrars and registrars of births and deaths. By the end of September 1838, 2,193 registrars had been appointed and, by the end of the year, 619 superintendent registrars.

Copies of this notice, announcing the establishment of registration districts, were affixed to the doors of every church and chapel in the Windsor Union.

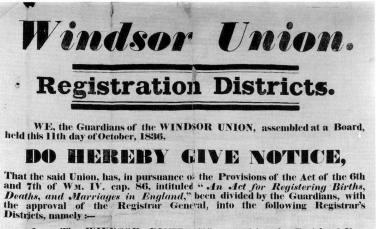

Windsor Union.

Registration Districts.

WE, the Guardians of the WINDSOR UNION, assembled at a Board, held this 11th day of October, 1836,

DO HEREBY GIVE NOTICE,

That the said Union, has, in pursuance of the Provisions of the Act of the 6th and 7th of Wm. IV. cap. 86, intituled "*An Act for Registering Births, Deaths, and Marriages in England,*" been divided by the Guardians, with the approval of the Registrar General, into the following Registrar's Districts, namely :—

1. "The WINDSOR DISTRICT," comprising the Parish of New Windsor, the Hamlet of Dedworth, the Parish of Clewer, and such parts of the Parishes of Old Windsor and Egham as lie North and East of the road leading from the Thames, near Leatherlake House, up Priest Hill, through Bishopsgate and Hardiman's Gate to the 23rd milestone on the Reading Road.

2. "The EGHAM DISTRICT," comprising such parts of the Parishes of Egham and Old Windsor as lie South and West of the road leading from the Thames, near Leatherlake House, up Priest Hill, through Bishopsgate and Hardiman's Gate, to the 23rd milestone on the Reading Road, the Parish of Sunninghill, and the Parish of Thorpe.

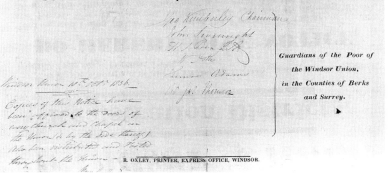

Guardians of the Poor of
the Windsor Union,
in the Counties of Berks
and Surrey.

R. OXLEY, PRINTER, EXPRESS OFFICE, WINDSOR.

Registrars, being Officers of a Poor Law Union.				Registrars, *not* being Officers of a Poor Law Union.					
Medical Officers.	Relieving Officers.	Other Officers.	Total.	In the Medical Profession.	In other Professions.	In Trade.	Not included in the three preceding Columns.	Total.	Total.
416	500	105	1021	111	262	437	362	1172	2193

The number of registrars appointed by 30 September 1838.
(*First Report of the Registrar General, 1837*)

In the early nineteenth century when roads and methods of transport were very different from what we know today, the size of the district, or sub-district, was critically important. The original church registration system was parochial so informants had only to travel the limits of the parish, but when the districts were substituted for the parishes they on average contained seven parishes. In this first registration Act, the responsibility for seeing that births and deaths were registered was put on the registrar who, if he was to do his job properly, would in most cases have to travel either on foot or horseback to the individual houses where the events occurred. More than thirty years later, when he was reviewing the working of the system in his Annual Report for 1872, the Registrar General estimated that the average area of a sub-district was twenty six and a half square miles and the average population 10,347 but that there was considerable variation between the different areas, the Poor Law Commissioners and Guardians having divided the country 'apparently without any very definite rule as to size or population'. He went on to note that 'the extremes are very wide from the average. The sub-district of Berwick-street, St James's, London comprises only 24 acres (0.0375 mile), while Bellingham in Northumberland, round the tributaries of the North Tyne comprises 175,131 acres (274 square miles)' and concluded that 'If the registrars visit every house to register births and deaths, they cannot on average travel more than two miles in each case nor probably much less than one mile unless they arrange to register the births periodically in beats'.

The superintendent registrar was responsible for examining and publishing the notices which could enable a marriage to proceed. He was also the person able to celebrate, according to prescribed form, the marriages of those who wanted a purely civil ceremony. The arrangements for civil marriage did not affect existing arrangements whereby the Church of England (and the Church in Wales) solemnised and registered their own marriages, nor did it affect the Society of Friends, 'commonly called Quakers', and Jews. Although other religious denominations were entitled to

The new Marriage Act. A young lady in the south of England in 1837 gives an account of the marriage of her sister in a Dissenting Chapel.
(Published in the *Bradford Observer*, 17 August 1837)

You know I was by no means disposed to leave the old church, or that my sister should be married any other way than our grandmothers were. I have often told her I could never *fancy* her really married, unless the knot were tied by a minister in a surplice. For two or three weeks past I teazed her about the insertion of her name in the Notice Book, and advised her to wear a veil before, as well as after, marriage. But she bore my raillery with wonderful patience; nay, she could laugh as well as I, and said that, for her part, she did not see why we need retain the marriage form our grandmothers used, any more than their bridal dresses, their hoops and high-heeled shoes. As her lover had long been a Dissenter, it would certainly have been rather inconsistent for them to have been married at Church . . . We were at the chapel by a little after eight . . . The whole service occupied not quite a quarter of an hour, during which, I assure you it never once occurred to me that neither surplice nor gown was to be seen . . . As this is the first Dissenting marriage in the parish, it has made a little stir; indeed nothing else is talked about. One of the servants tells me that the grocer thinks it will be necessary for the vicar to advertise his old concern, or the new shop, which has started so well will be likely to run away with the trade.

apply for their buildings to be registered for marriage ceremonies, a registrar of the district had to be present to register the actual marriage. By the end of 1838, 817 such registrars had been appointed, of whom 419 were also registrars of births and deaths.

The Poor Law Boards of Guardians were required to provide and equip register offices for the superintendent registrars but registrars had to provide their own accommodation. There had already been strong criticism of the choice of the Poor Law Unions as registration districts even before the passing of the 1836 Act and the inevitable close association of the superintendent registrar's office with the workhouse gave further weight to the arguments. It was some while before solemnisation of marriage at the new register offices was accepted, particularly in districts with strong religious ties. In Swansea, for example, the first two civil marriages are dated 9 October and 25 November, 1837, some four to five months after the start of the service, and in both cases the ceremonies were for two elderly widowed couples.

Below right, Lewisham gets its first register office.
(Published in the *Magazine of the Registration Service, 1972*.) Below, this extract from *The Times* editorial on 15 February 1836 reflects some of the early misgivings about the choice of the Poor Law Unions as registration districts.

We are of opinion, that whether from pride or from prejudice, or from other feeling, the strength of which it will not be prudent for the Legislature to contemn, the middle classes of the community will very much dislike to make personal applications at the *workhouses* of the districts in which they live for those certificates which are rendered necessary by the bill, before they can enter into the married state. We doubt also whether the Dissenters, and especially the *beau sexe*, will choose to have their marriage party or procession proceed to chapel under the escort of the overseer or relieving-officer (or whatever else the poor law functionary may be called), just after the fashion of the old pauper weddings, where the parish beadle was the most conspicuous personage in the group.

In 1836, with the passing of the Registration Acts, it became necessary to provide a Register Office, and the Guardians decided this could best be done by converting their Board Room. At a cost of £200 a "strong-closet" with brick lining and stone shelving was built into the rear wall of the Board Room and provided with iron doors. The Board Room served not only as the Register Office but also as the private office of the Clerk to the Board, and although there was a communicating door to the quarters of the Master of the Workhouse, at least it had its own entrance distinct from that to the Workhouse proper.

THE REGISTRATION OF BIRTHS AND DEATHS, AND THE MARRIAGE ACTS.

Yesterday a full meeting of the board of directors and guardians of the poor of Marylebone took place for the purpose of electing a superintendent-registrar, and for registering officers to do the parish duty under the above acts. This being the first metropolitan district in which such proceedings have taken place, in anticipation of these measures, a great number of strangers were attracted to the workhouse by the novelty of the scene.

Mr. WADMORE was in the chair.

The candidates were—Messrs. H. C. Wilson, Clapp, Kensett, Sinclair, Bell, Baxter, Staines, and Boys. The election was decided by ballot, though from the popularity of some of the candidates, and the previously expressed sentiments of many members of the board, scarcely a doubt existed as to who were to be the appointed individuals. Having drawn forth the votes, the chairman announced the returns as follows :—Mr. Wilson to be superintendent-registrar and marrying officer ; Mr. Kensett, to be registar for the district of All Souls and Trinity, which contains 3,380 houses and 34,000 inhabitants ; Mr. Bell, for the rectory division, containing 900 houses and 30,000 inhabitants ; Mr. Clapp, for St. Mary's district, containing 2,760 houses and 26,300 inhabitants ; and Mr. Baxter, to be registrar for Christchurch, the fourth and last district, containing 4,150 houses and 31,500 inhabitants.

The fortunate candidates returned thanks, and promised to discharge their respective duties with fidelity and diligence.

It is said that the situation of the superintendent-registrar will be worth at least 300*l.* a-year. His income will be derived from 2d. out of every shilling paid to the registrars, and from the licensing and matrimonial fees by parties who shall esteem marriage a civil compact rather than a sacred rite. The rest of the superintendent's salary will be paid out of the Consolidated Fund. The district registrars will have about 120*l.* a-year each, with prospects of increase. The fees will be for the first 20 certificates of birth and burial, 2s. 6d. each ; and for all subsequent ones 1s. each, the rest to be paid out of the poor-rates.

The births and marriages in Marylebone average 7,000 yearly.

The Board of Directors and Guardians of the Poor appointing a superintendent registrar in Marylebone in 1836. (Published in *The Times*, 21 September 1836)

Remuneration of the registration officers was by fee according to the number of entries made, for certified copies of these entries and for celebration of, or attendance at, marriages[1]. Before he could grant any licence for marriage, a superintendent registrar also had to give security 'by his Bond, in the Sum of One Hundred Pounds, to the Registrar General, for the due and faithful execution of his office'. A report in *The Times* on 21 September 1836, describing a meeting of the Board of Directors and

Guardians of the Poor of Marylebone to choose a superintendent registrar 'to do the parish duty' under the Acts, claimed that the income might be a substantial £300 per year, derived from 9d out of every shilling paid to the registrars and from the licensing and matrimonial fees 'by parties who shall esteem marriage a civil rather than a sacred rite'; the rest of the salary would be paid out of the Consolidated Fund. The registrars were paid half-a-crown for the first twenty entries of births and deaths in a calendar year and a shilling an entry thereafter.

The 'substantial £300 a year' for superintendent registrars was soon being questioned, partly because of the disparity in income between different types of area. Rural areas, for example, were large in size but thinly populated, so yielding only a small fee income. At the beginning of 1840, the Registrar General was already writing to the Marquess of Normanby, Secretary of State for the Home Department, about 'the very small and inadequate amount of remuneration to Suptn. Regrs.' which in some cases he described as '.... a pittance as scarcely equals for a whole year what an agricultural labourer can earn in a fortnight.' He enclosed certified copies of the amounts received by superintendent registrars in the first year of registration in 42 districts, 'all under £4 and one of these only 17s/6d', and went on to say that it was unnecessary for him to comment 'upon the obvious inadequacy of such remuneration for offices of trust which cannot be satisfactorily filled but by persons of good education well trained in habits of business'.

This system of paying fees to registrars and appointment by the local Poor Law Boards of Guardians persisted for nearly a hundred years. As people moved and workloads shifted, the rewards became more inequitable and, in 1928, pressure from the registrars themselves led to a private member's Bill being introduced into the House of Commons providing for a salaried service. The Bill passed through all its stages in the House of Commons 'only to perish in another place in the rush of the last hours of the Session'. So explained the Minister of Health when introducing the Local Government Bill of 1929 which, when it became law, put all new appointments on a salaried basis but gave existing registrars the choice of remaining fee-paid if they wished. The last registrar appointed under the old system and still receiving fees was still in post until the early 1980s. The Act brought the appointment, pay and accommodation of the registration service under the local authorities but left the Registrar General with the power to dismiss the officers and instruct them in the performance of their registration duties.

Administration of the registration service

The 1836 Acts laid down that the registration system was to be directed by a Registrar General with a suitably staffed office in London. Furthermore it set out in broad outline the way in which the new service was to operate. The Registrar General was required to provide 'a sufficient number of register books for making entries of all births, deaths and marriages of His Majesty's subjects in England' in the precise form set out in the Schedules appended to the Act. Each register contained space for five hundred entries and when a volume was completed it was to be returned to the local superintendent registrar. It is interesting to note that in many small parishes where few marriages are solemnised the original registers are still in current use.

Local registrars were required to send copies of the entries in their registers in the preceding quarter to their superintendent registrars who, after verifying them, were to forward them to the Registrar General so enabling a national registry to be established. In his first Annual Report Thomas Lister describes the care he took to see that the procedure was properly and promptly carried out. He goes on to describe how the copies were checked and queries followed up before they were sorted and bound into volumes. The final part of the process was the preparation of a quarterly alphabetical index for the whole country for births, deaths and marriages separately. He reports that in the first year of registration, ending 30 June 1838, these twelve volumes contain no less than 958,630 entries. This achievement, in an age when there were no typewriters, telephones or computers, is all the more remarkable when measured against the sneers of one of the speakers, when the original Bill was discussed in the House of Lords in July 1836, who suggested that the proposal was practically

By the directions issued to Superintendent Registrars, of which I submit a copy in the Appendix, I have endeavoured to ensure regularity and promptness in the quarterly collection of Certified Copies, and the transmission of them to the General Register Office, the observance of a strict method being absolutely essential in operations of such magnitude executed by so great a number of persons. The Certified Copies transmitted hither every quarter by the Superintendent Registrars are collected by them from more than 14,000 persons charged with the duty of compiling the same. More than 80,000 separate papers, containing 847,149 entries have been thus transmitted, of which 739,737 (being all the entries of Births and Deaths, and such Marriages as are registered by the Registrar of Marriages) have been compared with the originals by the Superintendent Registrars, and certified to be correct.

The first Registrar General ensured strict observance of the arrangements for collecting and despatching Certified Copies.
(*First Report of the Registrar General, 1837*)

impossible, inasmuch as 'the Registrar General would have to receive in every year 88,000 separate papers all of which he must classify'.

Needless to say the postal system of the day led to communication problems. Thomas Parker, the superintendent registrar of Lewisham, was already writing to Thomas Lister in 1837 pointing out that, although the 3d pacquet post from London covered all Lewisham, he had several times had to go or send to the General Post Office in London to collect parcels because they were over the 4 oz limit. Later, on 3 March 1838, the certified copies for the December quarter were duly sent off, the five registrars having made a total of 74 birth entries and 128 death entries, while marriages in the parish churches totalled 58 entries. The copies did not arrive and were thought to be lost. Some heated correspondence took place between Thomas Parker and the Inspector of the Post Office and the packets were eventually discovered at the Twopenny Post Office, held back as they were overweight[2].

The Registration Act also set out rules for guaranteeing the safety of the registers. The Registrar General was to supply 'a sufficient number of strong iron boxes to hold the register books' and every such box was to 'be furnished with a lock and two keys, and no more'; one of the keys was to be kept by the registrar and the other by the superintendent registrar.

Acceptance of the new system

Thomas Lister reported that within three calendar months of his appointment he had furnished to the respective Guardians of every union, parish or place for which Boards of Guardians were then established, printed notices concerning the Registration Act. These notices were to be published 'by fixing them on the outside of the several churches or chapels, or other public and conspicuous buildings or places'. He went on to say that, having thus complied with the strict letter of the law, he then set out to fulfil its spirit by other means 'best calculated to counteract erroneous impressions which experience had shown to exist'.

The atmosphere of controversy in which the new registration system had come into operation continued for some time. A group of clergy even issued a poster warning the public that they would have nothing to do with the new Act as regards marriage. The Church was also distressed by the need to register births and deaths with the civil registrar and the consequent loss of status of

And be it enacted, that the Registrar General shall furnish to every superintendent registrar, for the use of the registrars under his superintendence, a sufficient number of strong iron boxes to hold the register books to be kept by such registrar; and every such box shall be furnished with a lock and two keys, and no more; and one of such keys shall be kept by the registrar, and the other key shall be kept by the superintendent registrar; and the register books of each district, while in the custody of the registrar, and not in use, shall be always kept in the register box, and the register box shall always be left locked.

Registration Act 1836, section 14

One of the statutory iron strong boxes used for holding the registers. This 1845 version was specially manufactured by Thomas Milner and Son. The advertisement reads 'Milner's Patent Double-Chambered Fire-Resistant Safes & Boxes'.

its baptism and burial registers. Many churchmen continued to argue that the church registers of baptisms were superior to the civil registers of births for legally identifying individuals because the Christian names inserted were more reliable and, in most cases, they included birth as well as baptism dates. Although the civil registers allowed for baptismal names to be included at a later date, very few additions were in fact made. Some clergy went so far as to issue handbills advising inhabitants of their parishes that, if the registrar came in person to register a birth then they should 'give correct answers to all his questions; but they are not obliged to go to him for this purpose, nor are they liable to any penalty for not getting their children registered by him'[3].

A glance at the early registers in a town such as Brighton shows that, in the districts where the more educated lived, most birth entries do in fact include the first names of the children. Thus the Kemptown district, which included in its first fifteen entries in 1837 a physician and surgeon, an artist, a lapidary and jeweller and a policeman, all the children registered were given first names. Moreover all those informing the registrar of the births could sign their own names. The person having the most difficulty with her signature seems to have been Mary Robins, described as a pork butcher, in whose house was born Mary Barnes, the child of a 'spinster' and a horsedealer. The St Peter's district of Brighton, on the other hand, appears to have been socially very different: among the first fourteen entries only four children were given names and half the informants signed with a mark only. However, at a later

Fanny Sharp, wife of a brewer's labourer in the St Peter's district of Brighton, registers the birth of her son, Septimus Harry Archibald Richard Percy, on 27 July 1883.

NOTICE

FURNISHED BY THE REGISTRAR GENERAL, UNDER THE PROVISIONS OF THE ACT

For Registering Births, Deaths, and Marriages, in England.

Acts required to be done by Persons who may be desirous of solemnizing MARRIAGE after 1st day of March, 1837, under the provisions of the Acts of the 6th & 7th of William IV. cap. 85 and 86.

1. PERSONS desirous of solemnizing Marriage according to the rites and ceremonies of the Church of England, may be so Married after publication of Banns, or by Licence, or by Special Licence as heretofore; or they may be Married (without publication of Banns, or by Licence, or Special Licence,) according to the rites and ceremonies of the Church of England, on production of a Certificate from the Superintendent Registrar of the District, to be obtained in the following manner, namely:—

One of the Parties intending Marriage must give notice under his or her hand, to the Superintendent Registrar of the District, within which the Parties shall have dwelt for not less than seven days then next preceding; or if they dwell in different Districts, they must give the like notice to the Superintendent Registrar of *each* District. The notice must be in the form of a Schedule which the Superintendent Registrar will furnish on being applied to, and must be filled up with the following particulars:—

> The Name and Surname of each of the Parties.
> Whether Bachelor or Widower, Spinster or Widow.
> Their respective Rank, Profession, or Calling.
> Whether minors, or of full age.
> Their respective dwelling places.
> Whether they have resided within the District more than one calendar month, or if not, how long.
> In what Church or Building the Marriage is to be solemnized.
> The District and County in which the other Party resides when they dwell in different Districts.

A Copy of such Notice will be entered by the Superintendent Registrar in a book called "The Marriage Notice Book," which will be open at all reasonable times, without fee, to all persons desirous of inspecting the same.

The Notice must be read by the Superintendent Registrar, or by the Clerk to the Guardians, at three weekly meetings of the Guardians, or, if such meetings are not held weekly, at any meeting of the Guardians within twenty-one days from the day of the notice being entered in the Marriage Notice Book. And after the expiration of twenty-one days after the entry of the notice, if no impediment has been shewn, the Superintendent Registrar may be required to issue a Certificate.

2. Persons (except Quakers and Jews) desirous of solemnizing Marriage *not according* to the rites and ceremonies of the Church of England, may be Married according to *other* rites and ceremonies, on production of a Certificate obtained as above mentioned, *in a registered place of worship*, provided that every such Marriage shall be solemnized with open doors, between the hours of Eight and Twelve in the forenoon, in the presence of some Registrar of the District in which such registered building is situate, and of two or more credible witnesses; provided also that in some part of the Ceremony, and in the presence of such Registrar and witnesses, each of the Parties shall declare, as follows:—

"I do solemnly declare that I know not of any lawful impediment why I, A. B., may not be joined in matrimony to C. D."
And each of the Parties shall say to the other,

"I call upon these persons here present to witness that I, A. B., do take thee, C. D., to be my lawful wedded [wife or husband]."
Provided also that there be no lawful impediment to the Marriage of such Parties.

Persons may be Married after *seven* days from the entry of the Notice, if by *Licence*, and after *twenty-one* days if *without* Licence. A Licence may be granted by the Superintendent Registrar; but only for Marriage in a registered building within his district, or in his Office; but before any Licence can be granted by him, one of the Parties intending Marriage must appear personally before him, and in case he shall not be the Superintendent Registrar to whom notice of such intended Marriage was given, shall deliver to him the Certificate of the Superintendent Registrar, or Superintendent Registrars, to whom such Notice shall have been given; and such Party shall make oath, or shall make his or her solemn affirmation or declaration, instead of taking an oath, that he or she believeth that there is not any Impediment of Kindred or Alliance, or other lawful Hindrance to the said Marriage, and that one of the said Parties hath for the space of fifteen days immediately before the day of the Grant of such Licence had his or her usual place of abode within the District within which such Marriage is to be solemnized, and, where either of the Parties, (not being a Widower or Widow,) shall be under the Age of Twenty-one years, that the consent of the Person or Persons whose consent to such Marriage is required by Law has been obtained thereto, or that there is no Person having authority to give such consent, as the case may be.

3. Persons objecting to be Married either according to the rites and ceremonies of the Church of England, or in any such registered building, may, after Notice and Certificate as aforesaid, solemnize Marriage at the Office of the Superintendent Registrar, with open doors between the hours of Eight and Twelve in the forenoon, in the presence of the Superintendent Registrar and some Registrar of the District, and in the presence of two witnesses, making the declaration, and using the form of words required in the case of Marriage in a registered building.

Quakers may contract and solemnize Marriage according to the usages of their Society, provided both Parties are of that Society, that Notice shall have been given to the Superintendent Registrar, and a Certificate shall have been issued as before-mentioned.

Jews may likewise contract and solemnize Marriage according to the usages of the Jewish Religion, under similar provisions.

Every Marriage of which Notice has been entered as aforesaid must be solemnized within three calendar months after such entry, or the same must be renewed.

Every Marriage solemnized after the 1st of March, 1837, under the provisions of this Act for Marriages in England, in any other manner than as hereinbefore directed, will be null and void.

Be it also particularly observed that if any valid Marriage shall be had under the provisions of the Act for Marriages in England by means of any wilfully false Notice, Certificate, or Declaration made by either Party to such Marriage, as to any matter to which a Notice, Certificate, or Declaration is therein required, His Majesty's Attorney-General or Solicitor General may sue for a forfeiture of all estate and interest in any property accruing to the offending Party by such Marriage; and the proceedings and the consequences will be the same as are provided in the like case with regard to Marriages by Licence before the passing of these Acts.

Authority:—J. Hartnell, Fleet Street, London.

date in the St Peter's district, Fanny Sharp, the wife of a brewer's labourer, clearly gave great thought to her son's name and, nearly six weeks after the birth, in deference to the family name of Sharp, she registered him as Septimus Harry Archibald Richard Percy.

Despite the initial objections of the church and the scepticism of the public in general, by the time Thomas Lister died, on 5 June 1842, the registration service had been in existence nearly five years and was well established and accepted. It is a great tribute to his remarkable administrative gifts that the service has stood the test of time and remains in many respects unchanged today.

References

1. R K Freeman. An Outline of the Finances of the Local Registration Services from 1837, in the *Magazine of the Registration Service*, January 1972, No. 10.

2. L W Roache. Lewisham, the Evolution of a District, in the *Magazine of the Registration Service*, October 1972, No. 13.

3. William Atkinson, Rector of Gateshead Fell, 6th March 1839. Typed copy sent to Roger Thatcher with an accompanying letter from Cynthia Brown, superintendent registrar of Keighley, 10 June 1982.

The civil registration system

3

Setting up an inspectorate

When George Graham succeeded Thomas Lister in 1842, he inherited a system which was already well established but which needed developing and exploiting. In certain areas too it needed stiffening and rather more legal backing. Very soon after he took office the new Registrar General wrote to the Home Secretary, in December 1843, saying he was concerned about the discreditable state of some of the register offices, particularly the lack of security of their registers, and that he had had to dismiss four registrars. He proposed that four inspectors should be appointed. The Treasury decided that the appointments should be for one year only at a salary of £300 per annum with an allowance for 'tavern expenses' and four guineas a week for travelling expenses.

One of the problems was that the system of paying registrars by the entry was a temptation to unscrupulous ones to make fictitious entries. In the All Soul's district of Marylebone between 1840 and 1844 this was carried on to such a scale that it led to recalculation of the district's birth rate and prosecution of the registrar for felony. Elsewhere, in the Great Howard district of Liverpool where the registrar was prosecuted for a similar offence, the magistrate decided that the matter would have to go for trial and was such a serious matter that bail could not be granted. At the trial the defendant was found guilty by the jury and sentenced to six months' imprisonment with hard labour[1]:

The magistrate took the view that it was a grave matter, and as a felony must go for trial. Mr Chubb requested bail.
Mr Snowball – I'm afraid I shall have to oppose it. It is a felony, a very serious felony. There are many more cases.
Magistrate – More cases have you?
Mr Snowball – Oh dear, yes, a great many more.
Magistrate – I shall not take bail, then, under those circumstances. The prisoner stands remanded until to-morrow.

Prosecution of Mr Chubb, Registrar for the Great Howard District of Liverpool, September 1844.

Registration of births

One of the early problems of the service was enforcement of registration of births and deaths. Responsibility was placed on the

The clergy are no doubt excessively annoyed by the passing of this
[Registration] Act which not only deprives them of some of their
importance, but will likewise diminish their emoluments; but we question
the policy of their endeavour to thwart the operation of the Act . . . let these
gentry read the following case brought before the Leeds magistrates
yesterday, and be wise in time . . .

The whole question turned upon the point whether a paper given to
one of the Registrars was such a notice as was required by the Act—the
paper only stated, that on such a day [the day on which the deceased
William Pinkney was interred] the rev. gentleman had interred a dead body.
It contained no further description as to name or residence, or anything
that could lead the Registrar to the knowledge of any facts he would be
required to register. After a patient investigation of the case, the
magistrates decided, that there was not sufficient notice given of the burial
within the time required by the Act of Parliament and convicted the rev.
gentleman in the penalty of 10l., but it was afterwards mitigated to 5l. 5s.

registrar rather than the informant who could only be prosecuted if
he refused to give information after being requested to do so by the
registrar. Deaths registration was less of a problem than births
because no body could be buried without notification. In the case
of births, it was much more difficult to ensure that the parents or
other persons present at the event informed the registrar. A
number of prosecutions however were brought, such as that at the
Norfolk Summer Assizes in 1838 when Sophia Reeve, wife of
J Reeve of Shottesham, was prosecuted for refusing after request
to give information to the registrar touching the birth of her child.
The prosecution, on behalf of the Registrar General, said that the
registrar had gone to the defendant but she positively refused to
give the information he required. He went on to say that 'In the
present case . . . he feared that persons in a better sphere of life
than the defendant(s), were the advisers and instigators of a
contumacious course'. Sophia Reeve pleaded guilty but said that
her child had been properly registered at church.

The Registrar General, in his seventh Annual Report for
1843–44, admitted that in the early years many births had escaped
notice 'as parents are not bound to give information of a birth
unless requested to do so by the registrar'; latterly, he says, 'by
increased vigilance and better arrangements, the defects have
much diminished'. The Births and Deaths Registration Act of
1874 made enforcement easier by transferring the onus of
registration from the registrar to the parents, or occupier of the
house, or persons having charge of the child. It also tightened up
registration of illegitimate births by allowing the insertion of the
putative father's name only where the father attended before the
registrar with the mother and gave information jointly with her.

REGISTRATION OF BIRTHS.

NORFOLK SUMMER ASSIZES, 1838.

Before the Honourable Sir Joseph Littledale, one of Her Majesty's Justices of the Court of Queen's Bench.

IN this case the Grand Jury found a true bill against the defendant Sophia Reeve, wife of J. Reeve of Shottesham, within the Henstead District, for refusing after request to give information to the Registrar touching the birth of her child.

The defendant having surrendered herself and pleaded guilty to the indictment,...

... Upon being asked what she had to say for herself, the defendant said that she did not know there was any necessity for giving information; her child had been properly registered at Church.

Mr. Justice Littledale in passing sentence said, he fully believed the defendant when she expressed her ignorance of the consequences to which she had subjected herself. It was his duty to tell her that she had transgressed against an Act of Parliament, and that *it would be in his power to sentence her to be imprisoned for a year. This ought to be known to others to prevent their falling into the same error.* She was the first person who had been proceeded against in this district, and a favourable construction would be put upon her case, but *a repetition of the offence would be more seriously visited.* The Act for Registration of Births, &c., contained some wholesome provisions, and certainly not of a vexatious kind, as the father and mother were only called upon to give particulars of the birth of a child when the information was required of them. The defendant was here to answer to a charge of having refused to give that information. He recommended her to communicate to her neighbours the leniency with which she had been treated, at the same time assuring them that *those who in future knowingly and wilfully disobeyed this law, and refused to give information, would receive pretty severe punishment.* He should now sentence her to four days imprisonment, and as that reckoned from last Saturday, she would be immediately discharged, but he advised her not to come again.

J. HARTNELL, Red Lion Court, Fleet Street.

An account of the prosecution of Sophia Reeve at the Norfolk Assizes, 1838, for failing to give the registrar details about the birth of her child.

Previously the mother of an illegitimate child might name whom she pleased as the father and the registrar was bound to accept her information. The Act provided for penalties and modified the fees charged for late registrations.

The main difference between a birth certificate today and that of 150 years ago is that, since 1969, the mother's usual address is given and also place of birth of the father and the mother is given as well as that of the child. Since 1986 occupational details have been included for the mother as well as the father. A very important change however was introduced by the Population (Statistics) Act, 1938, which although it did not alter the form of the standard birth certificate itself, greatly increased the amount of information which the registrar asked confidentially of the informant and which he then included on a draft form only. This draft served both the purpose of checking the information given before it was entered in the birth register and also as a basic document for central statistical processing. The additional information included the age of the mother and, for legitimate births, the parents' date of marriage and the number of previous live and still births to the mother within marriage. It did not provide for details of previous illegitimate births. In 1960 a further Act provided for the age of the father to be included where the father's name is recorded in the register. The significance of the Acts and the additional information which they made possible are discussed in a later chapter on population (Chapter 11).

Much later, in 1947, provision was made for a shortened form of birth certificate in addition to the standard one. It shows only the name, sex, date and place of birth of the child, and therefore does not disclose any details of parentage. During the past sixty years various Acts have been passed legitimating children on the subsequent marriage of their parents and provision has been made for re-registering the birth to show the child's new status.

A number of Acts have modified and regularised the position of adopted children and, in 1927, an Adopted Children Register was set up by the Registrar General to record all legal adoptions. For each entry in that register the corresponding birth record is marked 'Adopted'. Disclosure of the link between the adoption entry and the original birth entry is forbidden, except in certain circumstances, and the short birth certificate from the Adopted Children Register is in the same form as a similar certificate from the birth records.

Registration of marriages

The marriage certificate today is the same as it was 150 years ago and, as already mentioned, many churches are still using their as yet uncompleted original registers. The pages of these registers, and those held in local registry offices reveal snapshots of local and national history. The Brighton register for example contains the signature of David Livingstone, the missionary and explorer, who witnessed the marriage in 1858 at the Union Street Chapel of John Smith Moffatt, also a missionary and son of Robert Moffatt who is described in the register as a South African missionary. In the

Snapshots of local and national history. Below, a marriage entry showing the signature of David Livingstone, witnessing the marriage of fellow-missionary John Smith Moffatt. Opposite, the entry recording the marriage in 1930 of the Archduke of Austria and Prince of Hungary to Irene Rudnay.

No.	When Married.	Name and Surname.	Age.	Condition.	Rank or Profession.	Residence at the time of Marriage.	Father's Name and Surname.	Rank or Profession of Father.

19 *30*. Marriage solemnized at *the Register Office*
in the District of *Brighton* in the County of *Brighton*

Columns:—	1	2	3	4	5	6	7	8
218	*Sixteenth August 1930*	*Albrecht Franz Joseph Carl Friedrich Georg Hubert Maria Habsburg-Lothingen*	*33 years*	*Bachelor*	*Archduke of Austria Prince of Hungary*	*King's Hotel Brighton*	*Friedrich Habsburg-Lothingen*	*Archduke of Austria Prince of Hungary*
		Irene Dora Rudnay formerly Zelbach	*33 years*	*formerly the wife of Lewis Stephen Rudnay from whom she obtained a divorce*	—	*King's Hotel Brighton*	*John Zelbach (deceased)*	*Landed proprietor*

Married in the *Register Office* according to the Rites and Ceremonies of the _____ by *Licence* before me,

This Marriage was solemnized between us, { *Archduke Albrecht* / *Irene Dora Rudnay* } in the Presence of us, { *J. de Hove* / *G. S. Goofer* } *G. H. Morrison, Registrar* *Ernest Infield Supt. Regr.*

present century, in August 1930, there is recorded the marriage in Brighton Register Office itself of 33 year-old Albrecht Franz Joseph Carl Friedrich Georg Hubert Maria Habsburg-Lothingen, Archduke of Austria and Prince of Hungary, to Irene Dora Rudnay described as 'formerly the wife of Lears Stephen Rudnay from whom she obtained a divorce'. A report on the wedding in *The Daily Express* described how the Archduke renounced all claims to the Hungarian crown for the sake of this lady who was previously married to the Hungarian Minister of State in Sofia.

In 1862, Thomas Parker, the superintendent registrar in Lewisham, found himself slightly nonplussed when faced with the first re-marriage of a divorced woman: being uncertain how the lady's marital status should be described, he wrote to the Registrar General for advice.

Although attitudes to marriage have changed fundamentally, there have been comparatively few changes in marriage procedures themselves since the Marriage Act in 1836. One of the most important was in the Marriage Act of 1898 which authorised Dissenting congregations to appoint an 'authorised person' to register marriages so allowing them to dispense with the attendance of the registrar, an obligation which many had resented because it put them in an inferior position to those marrying in the Church of England or the Church in Wales. The ceremonies however still had to take place in a registered building, the only exception being for Jews and Quakers who had been specifically exempted in the 1836 Act. It was not until the Marriage Act of 1970 that provision was made for marriage by a licence issued by the Registrar General in unlicensed premises in exceptional circumstances, such as where one of the parties was seriously ill and could not be expected to recover and could not be moved to a place where marriages are normally solemnised. A recent example was the marriage of the actress Pat Phoenix, of Granada TV series

'Marriage by Registrar'. An engraving by W B Boucher based on a painting by W Dendy Sadler (1854–1923). The picture is thought to represent a marriage in St Ives (Hunts) Register Office, and the original painting probably dates from about 1900.

'Coronation Street' fame, who was critically ill with lung cancer in the Alexandra Hospital at Cheadle near Manchester, and was married to actor Tony Booth at a ceremony in her hospital room. The Marriage Act of 1983 went further by making it possible for the marriage of a house-bound or detained person (such as those in prison) to take place where that person resides.

One of the more significant social changes in the present century has been the raising of the minimum age of marriage in 1929 from 12 years for girls and 14 for boys to 16 for both parties. In 1969 the Family Law Reform Act reduced the age of majority from 21 years to 18, and this then became the minimum age of marriage without parental consent.

The most recent legislation, the Marriage Act of 1986, has further lifted restrictions on people who may marry each other. The original Marriage Act of 1836, 150 years before, based its rules on the practice of the Church of England. set out in the Prayer Book in what was known as Archbishop Parker's Table. This table was taken from the Code of Canons prepared for the Reformed Church and was derived from the book of Leviticus in the Bible. It declared that any marriages which breached the impediments were 'incestuous and unlawful and consequently shall be dissolved from the beginning'. In 1907 a Marriage Act made it lawful for a man to marry his deceased wife's sister and another, in 1960, his divorced wife's sister. The 1986 Act permitted marriage with a step-child or step-grandchild, provided that both parties are 18 years of age at the time of the marriage and the younger party must never, while under the age of 18 years, have been treated as a child of the other's family.

Today, unlike 1837, the marriage ceremony in a register office is accepted by rich and poor alike. It no longer carries the stigma of the Poor Law office. Moreover the looser hold of religion in present society along with the steadily rising number of marriages which are second or third marriages for one or both partners have increased the popularity of civil ceremonies. Almost a half of all marriages are now solemnised before a superintendent registrar. Of the rest, about two thirds are conducted by the clergy of the Church of England and the Church in Wales. They remain in the privileged position given to them by the Marriage Act of 1836 which allowed them to dispense with civil preliminaries in favour of ecclesiastical ones and only notify the local registrar when quarterly copies of the church register are subsequently sent to the

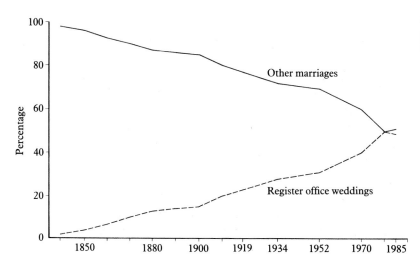

Chart 3.1   Changes in the proportion of civil and religious ceremonies, England and Wales, 1850–1985.

local registry office. The remaining small group of marriage ceremonies mostly occupy a half-way position: they are subject to civil preliminaries but, provided the buildings in which the marriages take place are registered, the registration of the marriage is carried out in the same place by a person authorised to do so. There has been some pressure to simplify the procedure by giving the responsibility to an authorised person without reference to a building and it should be noted that this is the system prevailing in Scotland. Scotland too grants no special privileges to the Established Church and demands that all marriages be preceded by civil preliminaries.

Registration of deaths

Death certificates have undergone greater change. In 1837 the only details the informant was asked for were date of death, name and surname, age, sex, rank or profession and cause of death of the deceased. Today the register also includes place of death, date and place of birth, usual address and, in the case of a woman who has married, her maiden surname. One of the most important changes was brought about by the Births and Deaths Registration Act of 1874 which transferred the onus of registration from the registrar to the nearest relative of the deceased. The Act also made it compulsory for registration to be supported by a medical certificate specifying causes of death and signed by the medical practitioner who attended the dead person during their final illness. The form of certificate was altered in 1927: the new certificate was in two parts, the first for causes leading to death and the second for other causes influencing death but not its main cause. Since 1949 greater detail has been required about those causes. Meanwhile in 1926 registration of still births was made compulsory. As in the case of births registration, the Population (Statistics) Act of 1938 required important additional information about the deceased person and the registrar includes in a confidential draft entry further particulars relating to the marital status of the deceased and their employment status.

The importance of death certificates for medical research was understood long before the 1836 Act came into force. A letter in *The Times* in October 1836 drew attention to the deficiency of medical statistics in this country compared with many other countries in Europe and pleaded for medical men to be appointed registrars. Thomas Lister was very well aware of the importance of obtaining 'a faithful statement of the cause of Death in the column

Penal servitude for giving false information to the registrars.

CAUTION.

CONVICTION FOR GIVING FALSE INFORMATION TO A REGISTRAR OF BIRTHS AND DEATHS.

At the Anglesey Assizes, held before Lord Chief Justice Coleridge, at Beaumaris, on 24th July, 1875, T— M— H— was indicted under the 36th Section of 24 and 25 Vict., Cap. 98, for feloniously giving to the Registrar of the Sub-District of Beaumaris, **False Information** respecting the Death of Ernest Hamer, and thereby causing a **False Entry** of such Death to be made in the Register Book.

The Prisoner having been found **GUILTY**, was sentenced to **FIVE YEARS PENAL SERVITUDE.**

of the register set apart for that purpose' and he sent a circular address to all authorised Practitioners of Medicine and Surgery in England and Wales – whose addresses he was able to obtain – entreating them to give an authentic name of the fatal disease. George Graham, his successor, reported in the seventh Annual Report in 1843–44 that he had again appealed to all authorised medical practitioners to give written statements of the cause of death and he had furnished them with books of blank certificates for the purpose. In many cases, of course, doctors did not attend people who died and the registrars were then faced with the problem of accepting what the informants told them. Thus John Williams, a youth of 18, described as a shoemaker living at the Three Grapes, Llanrhidian, died in April 1849 of the 'King's Evil, 4 years'.

There still remained the difficulty of analysing causes of death because of inconsistency in the basic information. The solution to this problem, the development by William Farr of a 'nosology', or list of morbid conditions, is described in Chapter 9, on health statistics.

In the seventh Annual Report the Registrar General also called the attention of coroners to the importance of giving details of the causes of violent deaths, particularly with a view to preventing accidents by improved safety measures. Some of the

I have also called the attention of coroners to the importance of returning, in all fatal cases inquired into by juries, the causes of violent deaths, more accurately and more in detail than has, except in a few cases, been done hitherto, in the hope that, when these causes are determined and carefully analyzed, means may be devised for guarding against their effects, for throwing additional security around human life, improving the public health, preventing crime, and advancing medical science.

The Registrar General stresses the importance of recording full and accurate details on the cause of violent deaths.
(*Seventh Report of the Registrar General, 1843*)

records of accidental deaths are a poignant reminder of the social conditions prevailing in the nineteenth century. An excerpt from a page of the Swansea register in 1854 shows the accidental deaths of two boys, aged eleven and thirteen, who were working underground in the pits and, on the same page, there is recorded the accidental death of a stone-mason who was still working at the age of 74 and was 'killed by a blow from the bob of a steam engine'.

The Swansea register also records, in 1858, the death of a Greek seaman who was 'murdered by stabbing'. Three weeks later there is recorded the 'execution for wilful murder' of the two Greek seamen who killed him. They were publicly hanged and the local press reports how on the day before the execution, 'thousands of the lower orders' flocked into the town, and in the district

No.	When Died.	Name and Surname.	Sex.	Age.	Rank or Profession.	Cause of Death.
	1854. DEATHS in the *District* of *Llandilotalybout*					
461	Ninth March 1854 Tyrcamol Colliery Llangafelach	John Jenkins	Male	74 Years	Stone Mason	Accidentally killed by a blow from the Bob of a steam Engin —
462	Twentyeighth August 1854 Lone Colliery Llangafelach	John Morgan	Male	11 Years	Horse driver in Colliery	Crushed between Tram waggon and the coal by the waggon accidentally running against him
463	Second November 1854 Mynythnewith Colliery Llangafelach	David Cornelius	Male	13 Years	Horse driver in Colliery	Killed by Tram waggon accidentally over his Body

Accidental deaths, recorded in 1854 in the Swansea deaths register.

adjacent to the scaffold, many score of showmen, boothsmen and gamblers took up their station for the night[2].

The Swansea register of deaths also records the last public hanging in Britain of a murderer. This took place in January 1866, just over 120 years ago, on the same spot as that of the two Greek seamen, when a 19 year-old youth was executed for the murder of his friend. On this occasion it was estimated that a crowd of 15,000 were present. The police had great difficulty in maintaining order and it was reported that in the surging crowds women and children were trampled underfoot and 120 injured. The subsequent outcry against capital punishment was one of the main factors leading to the decision to carry out future executions in private[3].

Execution for wilful murder, Swansea 1858
(W W Hunt, *A History of the Swansea Police Force*)

We regret to say that the major part of these people seem to flock to such scenes as though they were about to witness some great national sport of former days—their levity and profane demeanor is disgusting and disgraceful to very true-hearted Englishman. One showman reaped a considerable sum by suspending over his show a painted board containing the words, correct portraits of the murderers may be seen within.

The death entry of the last murderer to be publicly hanged, January 1866

Twelfth April 1866 H M Gaol Swansea	Robert Coe	Male	19 Years	Collier	Executed	William Coe present at the death H M Gaol Swansea

The present and the future

The administration of registration changed very little until the Local Government Act of 1929 transferred the Poor Law functions to county or borough councils. Their functions under the previous registration Acts were also transferred to local authorities but the Registrar General retained general responsibility for the administration of the registration service. Today 117 local authorities are responsible, between them, for 416 registration districts, and these are staffed by nearly 2,000 registration officers and their deputies. Some offices, such as those in Bradford and Leicester, are housed in the very same buildings as under the Poor Law administration, although they have been much improved and refurbished. Other offices, such as Plymouth, Sheffield, Leeds and Hammersmith, enjoy modern, purpose-built accommodation.

The local offices handle nearly one and a half million registrations each year – some 600,000 each for births and deaths and 300,000 for marriages. The original registers for each district are held in the register office of that district and certificates can be issued from them. In total three and a half million are issued each year. As in 1837, every three months copies of all birth, marriage and death returns are sent to a central office, now the OPCS office in Titchfield, Hampshire, where they are checked, sorted into volumes and indexed. The volumes are filmed and the films then sent to be stored in St Catherines House in London and it is from these microfilmed records that certified copies of entries, stamped with the seal of the General Register Office, are issued to those people who apply at OPCS headquarters. There are now some 260 millions of these records dating back to 1837.

In most respects therefore the registration system is little different from 150 years ago. It is governed by a multiplicity of statutes enacted over the years to meet changing circumstances. The result often involves complex procedures which defy simple administration. Nonetheless, as a recent Government efficiency scrutiny report concluded, 'a combination of ingenuity, dedication and good-will enables [the service] to maintain impressively high standards of registration'[4].

Anyone who has been to a local register office to notify a birth or a death may have been surprised to find, in this day and age, that in many cases the registrar laboriously writes out by hand, not only the register entry itself, but also any copies that may be required. One of the reasons is that great care is taken, by using special paper and special ink, to ensure that the records are permanent and cannot be tampered with or fraudulently copied. It is perhaps equally surprising to discover that the search for a particular record is usually carried out manually. Computerisation has been slow to invade the registration service. A few years from now it may well be that local offices and OPCS headquarters itself will be transformed so that at least all new records and their indexes are kept on computers, either on a small scale at the local offices themselves or on a much bigger scale on a national data bank. The latter development could mean that all future registrations in any part of the country could be traced by any local office. Two of the big problems are reliability and security. One day too the Office may face up to the formidable and exceedingly costly task of transferring to a computer the 260 million existing records and their indexes, so avoiding the thumbing through of heavy volumes in the crowded search room of St Catherines House.

References

1.   P H Gibson. Some Curiosities from the Vaults, in the *Magazine of the Registration Service*, July 1972, No. 12.

2.   Walter William Hunt. *To Guard my People: a History of the Swansea Police Force*. 1957, Jones and Son, Morriston, Swansea.

3.   Hunt. Op. cit.

4.   *Efficiency Scrutiny Report on Registration of Births, Deaths and Marriages*. 1985, OPCS, London.

Social commentary

4

George Graham, like his predecessor Thomas Lister, was not only a good administrator but a master of language and a Registrar General with a keen social conscience. He was required, under the 1836 Acts, to prepare annually an abstract of the numbers of births, deaths and marriages registered and he and William Farr used these Annual Reports for some forty years to comment on current economic and social problems and to provoke action from government. The Registrar General also became responsible for carrying out the censuses of population and these too were used to probe social issues (see Chapter 6). In addition, in 1849, Graham instituted the *Quarterly Return* and, as the extract shows, he did this in the hope that policy decisions might be based on fact rather than hunch. (The *Quarterly Return* continued until 1975 when it was

An extract from the first *Registrar General's Quarterly Return*, published in 1849

The Marriages, Births and Deaths produce important effects; are influenced by the prosperity of the country; and express the hopes, fears, enjoyments, and sufferings of the people living in the agricultural, mining and manufacturing districts; on the coasts and in the interior of the country; in the narrow tortuous streets of cities, and in the sunshine and showers on hill sides and moors . . . As they are facts, and are expressed numerically, they admit of no exaggeration; while they correct the fallacy of judging of the state of a great and various kingdom either from the field of one man's experience – from his own parish and county – or from vague, accidental, prejudiced representations. The present arrangement will show, at short intervals, how many marry, how many are born, and how many die in England; and will thus appear in time to enable the public and the Legislature to take the indications which the returns may furnish into account in the conduct of affairs.

replaced by the quarterly publication *Population Trends* which, in addition to annual and quarterly statistics for all the main demographic series compiled by the Office, also included extended reports and commentaries on all OPCS activities.) *Weekly Returns* of burials were already in existence for London when the GRO was set up and shortly afterwards, in 1840, a weekly table was issued for the Metropolis showing the number of deaths by cause. Gradually other areas were included and, in his 27th Annual Report for 1874, the Registrar General commented that he had added 'weekly returns for the Outer Ring of London and for all the great cities of the United Kingdom'. From 1845 these weekly returns also covered births and since 1895 notifiable diseases.

The weekly table of mortality for the Metropolis, introduced by the GRO in 1840

A TABLE OF MORTALITY
FOR THE
𝕸etropolis,*
SHEWING THE NUMBER OF DEATHS FROM ALL CAUSES
Registered in the WEEK ending Saturday, the 18th January, 1840.

Causes of Death.	Age 0 to 15	Age 15 to 60	Age 60 and upwards	Total	Weekly Average, 1838
Small Pox	3	..	..	3	73
Measles	20	..	..	20	11
Scarlatina	47	4	..	51	29
Hooping Cough	20	1	..	21	40
Croup	5	..	..	5	7
Thrush	4	..	..	4	6
Diarrhœa	2	2	1	5	8
Dysentery	..	1	..	1	2
Cholera	..	..	..	..	.3
Influenza	2	1	..	3	1
Typhus (1)	9	9	9	27	78
Erysipelas	2	..	1	3	8
Syphilis	..	1	..	1	1
Hydrophobia	..	..	..	..	.2
Epidemic, Endemic, & Contagious Diseases	114	19	11	144	265
Cephalitis	6	5	..	11	10
Hydrocephalus	35	1	..	36	34
Apoplexy	1	4	8	13	19
Paralysis	1	6	14	21	14
Convulsions	55	1	..	56	67
Epilepsy	1	2	..	3	4
Insanity	..	1	1	2	1
Delirium Tremens	..	1	..	1	1
Dis. of Brain, &c. (2)	8	5	3	16	6
Diseases of the Brain, Nerves, and Senses.	107	26	26	159	156
Quinsey	1	1	..	2	2
Bronchitis	..	4	3	7	8
Pleurisy	..	1	..	1	2
Pneumonia	57	23	10	90	71
Hydrothorax	2	8	6	16	6
Asthma	1	32	33	66	28
Consumption	17	137	12	166	146
Dis. of Lungs, &c. (3)	6	13	6	25	10
Diseases of the Lungs, and other Organs of Respiration	84	219	70	373	275
Pericarditis	1	1	..	2	.3
Aneurism	..	..	..	..	.5
Dis. of Heart, &c. (4)	3	14	11	28	15
Diseases of the Heart and Bloodvessels.	4	15	11	30	16
Teething	18	..	..	18	15
Gastritis—Enteritis	6	8	1	15	17
Peritonitis	..	..	..	..	1
Tabes Mesenterica	3	..	..	3	3
Ascites	..	2	..	2	.4
Ulceration	..	..	..	..	1
Hernia	..	1	1	2	2
Colic or Ileus (5)	..	..	..	..	4
Dis. of Stomach, &c. (6)	1	3	1	5	4
Hepatitis	..	..	..	..	1
Jaundice	..	3	..	3	2
Dis. of Liver, &c. (7)	..	1	1	2	7
Diseases of the Stomach, Liver, and other Organs of Digestion	28	19	4	51	57

Causes of Death.	Age 0 to 15	Age 15 to 60	Age 60 and upwards	Total	Weekly Average, 1838
Nephritis	..	..	..	..	.5
Diabetes	..	..	..	..	.4
Stone	..	..	..	..	.4
Stricture	..	..	..	..	.6
Dis. of Kidneys, &c. (8)	..	3	..	3	3
Diseases of the Kidneys, &c.	..	3	..	3	5
Childbed	..	6	..	6	8
Ovarian Dropsy	..	..	..	..	.3
Dis. of Uterus, &c. (9)	..	1	..	1	2
Childbed, Diseases of the Uterus, &c.	..	7	..	7	10
Rheumatism	..	1	..	1	4
Dis. of Joints, &c. (10)	1	3	3	7	4
Diseases of the Joints, Bones and Muscles	2	3	3	8	8
Ulcer	1	..	1	2	.4
Fistula	..	..	..	..	.4
Dis. of Skin, &c. (11)	..	..	..	..	1
Diseases of the Skin, &c.	1	..	1	2	1
Inflammation	1	3	1	5	18
Hæmorrhage	..	2	..	2	4
Dropsy	3	21	15	39	34
Abscess	2	..	..	2	4
Mortification	1	1	1	3	4
Scrofula (12)	4	..	..	4	1
Carcinoma	..	3	1	4	6
Tumor	..	1	1	2	1
Gout	..	..	..	..	1
Atrophy	1	..	..	1	4
Debility	18	2	4	24	12
Malformations	..	..	..	..	1
Sudden Deaths	5	7	4½	17	12
Diseases of Uncertain Seat	35	40	27	103	102
Old Age, or Natural Decay	..	2	89	91	79
Intemperance	..	..	..	..	.4
Privation	..	..	..	..	.6
Violent Deaths	17	8	1	26	25
Death by Violence, Privation, or Intemperance	17	8	1	26	26
Causes not specified	..	..	..	..	13
Deaths from all Causes	392	361	244	997¾	
Weekly Average, 1838.	446	362	192	‡	1013

N.B.—The following Diseases, when they occur, are included under the heads of those to which the accompanying numerals are respectively subjoined.

(1) Ague. Remittent Fever.
(2) Tetanus, 1. Chorea, 1.
(3) Laryngitis, 1.
(4) Hypertrophy.
(5) Intussusception.
(6) Stricture of œsophagus. Hœmatemesis. Worms.
(7) Disease of Spleen.
(8) Ischuria, 1. Granular Disease.
(9) Paramenia.
(10) Arthritis.
(11) Carbuncle. Scald Head. Phlegmon.
(12) Purpura.

District		Deaths in the Week.	Average Weekly Deaths, 1838.
West Districts	Kensington; St. George, Hanover Square; Westminster; St. Martin in the Fields; St. James	160	156
North Districts	St. Mary-le-bone; St. Pancras; Islington; Hackney	170	172
Central Districts	St. Giles and St. George; Strand; Holborn; Clerkenwell; St. Luke; East London; West London; City of London	230	208
East Districts	Shoreditch; Bethnal Green; Whitechapel; St. George in the East; Stepney; Poplar	216	239
South Districts	St. Saviour; St. Olave; Bermondsey; St. George, Southwark; Newington; Lambeth; Camberwell; Rotherhithe; Greenwich	221	238
TOTAL. Males, 507. Females, 490. (Weekly average 1838, Male, 520. Females, 493.)		997	1013

* Under the term Metropolis are comprised the 32 Districts herein mentioned, which include the City of London *within*, and *without* the Walls, the City and Liberties of Westminster, the *Out Parishes* within the Bills of Mortality;—and the Parishes of St. Mary-le-bone; St. Pancras; Kensington; Fulham; Hammersmith (Chapelry); St. Luke, Chelsea; Paddington; St. Mary, Stoke Newington; St. Leonard, Bromley; St. Mary-le-bow; Camberwell; Greenwich; St. Nicholas, and St. Paul, Deptford; and Woolwich. The Population as enumerated in 1831, was 1,594,890.

† The Weekly Average for 1838 was obtained by dividing the Deaths Registered in that year by 52. In comparing it with the weekly Deaths in 1840, it must be borne in mind that the Metropolis increases nearly 2 per cent. annually; and that if the population had been the same in 1838 as in 1840, the Deaths would have been one 27th part more numerous. Decimals were employed only when less than one death occurred weekly.

‡ Age of 3 not stated, 1838. In the last week the age of one person, who died suddenly, was not stated.

General Register Office, Jan. 18th, 1840.

From time to time the GRO also conducted special surveys. For example, in 1842, Thomas Mann, chief clerk at the GRO, directed a circular on behalf of the Registrar General to the registrars in metropolitan districts enquiring about the sanitary conditions in their districts. The questions he asked are shown on page 40. In his covering letter he explained that he was not expecting them to conduct any special investigation into the circumstances referred to because he took it for granted that, as a consequence of carrying out their official duties, they were well enough acquainted with the sanitary conditions of their districts to provide the information needed. He went on to say that he hoped the answers would be 'sufficiently precise, accurate, and important to be employed in preparing a summary view of the health of the Metropolitan Districts'. He ended by saying that, if the space on the form was insufficient, they were at liberty to forward an additional written paper setting out 'all which you may desire to communicate'.

George Graham's first Annual Report covered the year ending 30 June 1841 when Thomas Lister was still Registrar General. Graham quickly recognised that much of the material which the GRO was gathering could be used as indicators of the state of society and he took as an example the proportion of people who were unable to sign the marriage register with their names and had to use a cross instead. He remarked that the average age of the parties who marry was about twenty-five years of age thus testing the level of education ten to twenty years previously. From the average of the last three years he reported that 33 men in 100 and 49 women in 100 signed their names in the marriage register with marks. He then went on to study the different counties and divisions of the country and prepared a table showing London with the lowest and Wales with the highest proportions signing with marks. In his Annual Reports he regularly commented on progress and, thirty-five years later, in 1876, he noted that 16 per cent of men and 22 per cent of women signed with a mark, a considerable improvement on the earlier situation. 'In the agricultural counties', he wrote, 'as a rule the women are better educated than the men but the converse of this is the case in the mining and manufacturing counties where the proportional number of women who signed with a mark was excessively high'.

George Graham's Annual Reports, particularly those during the 1870s, included social comments on a wide variety of topics, such as the prices of meat and cereals, the number of cattle and sheep, the supply of gold and the number of paupers receiving poor relief. He even went so far, in his report for 1848 when

An enquiry instituted in 1841 by the Registrar General, into the sanitary conditions in London
(*Fifth Report of the Registrar General, 1841*)

(CIRCULAR.)

Sir,   *General Register Office, October* 7, 1842.

I am directed by the Registrar General to transmit to you the enclosed Form of Return, with a request that you will insert in the blank space opposite to each Enquiry such statement in answer thereto as you may be able to make.

The Registrar General does not require that you should enter into any special investigation of the circumstances referred to in the enclosed queries ; he, however, takes it for granted that you are well acquainted with the sanatory condition of the district of which you are Registrar, and that in the discharge of your official duties many facts must have fallen under your notice tending to throw light on the cause of mortality. He wishes you, therefore, to embody the information in your possession under the respective heads in the enclosed Form of Return, and hopes that it will be sufficiently precise, accurate, and important to be employed in preparing a summary view of the health of the Metropolitan Districts. The limited space in the Form of Return will render great condensation in your statements necessary ; but you are at liberty to forward with it an additional written paper, if you have not space in the Form now sent to insert all which you may desire to communicate.

I am, Sir, your obedient Servant,

To   Thos. Mann, *Chief Clerk.*

The Registrar of Births and Deaths.

QUERIES.

1.—In what *parts* of your District has the number of deaths registered in the years 1838, 1839, 1840, 1841 and 1842 been the greatest in proportion to the Population ?

2.—In what *parts* of your District has the greatest number of deaths occurred from Small Pox, Measles, Scarlatina, Hooping Cough, Diarrhœa, Dysentery, Cholera, Influenza, or Fever (Typhus) ?
   a. And in what parts have Epidemic diseases been most fatal ?

3.—Name any particular *Streets, Courts,* or *Houses* which, from the number of deaths occurring therein, and the nature of the diseases, appear to you to be *unhealthy.*

4.—And state generally the condition of those unhealthy Streets, Courts, and Houses (No. 3),
   a. As to drainage.
      Supplies of Water.
      Cleanliness.
   b. Density of Population :—
      The number of persons sleeping in the same rooms, &c.
   c. State also the general condition of the population in those unhealthy Streets, Courts, or Houses (*e. g.*),
   d. What are their principal Occupations?
   e. Are their earnings comparatively high or low—regular or irregular ?
   f. Does their principal food consist of Potatoes, Bread, or Butchers' Meat ?
   g. Do they obtain little firing in Winter ?
   h. Are their habits temperate, or the reverse ?

5.—Name any particular Streets or parts which, according to the facts that have fallen under your notice, appear to you to be *healthy ;* and, with reference to the points adverted to in Question 4, compare the healthy with the unhealthy portions of your District.

The marriage registers have afforded a test of the state of education, with reference to writing. The simplicity of this test is one of its chief recommendations; the parties are neither asked whether they can write or read, nor formally requested to write; but sign the marriage registers with their name or their mark in attesting the marriage, and the tables show the proportion who signed with marks. The parties who marry are on an average about 25 years of age; so the test shows the state of education 10 or 20 years ago, and the subsequent inducements to the retaining of the information and skill then acquired.

It appears from the average of three years that 33 men in 100, and 49 women in 100 signed with marks: it is therefore probable that only 67 men and 51 women in 100 can write their own names. There is a slight increase in the proportion of men who wrote their names.

The value of this test . . . is questioned upon the ground that it is, in itself, no proof of education; and it must be at once admitted that at the utmost it shows only how many out of a given number can or cannot write. Many of the men and women who cannot now write, as in the days of old when barons and knights signed with marks, possess great intelligence and have acquired many useful arts; so thousands, on the other hand, who read and write, are ill educated, and know nothing of those liberal arts and sciences which enlarge, refresh, and invigorate the mind as the sunshine and showers fertilize and adorn the soil of England.

Number of persons who signed the marriage registers with marks.
(*Fourth Report of the Registrar General, 1840–1*)

The Registrar General ponders the meaning of education
(*Thirty-first Report of the Registrar General, 1868*)

discussing public health, as to include a brief homily about diets and remarked that 'Fruit, potatoes, and green vegetables are essential parts of the food of man, and it is only when taken to excess that, like other articles of diet, they disorder the stomach'. There were also regular reports on the weather, recording events such as the number days when snow fell, the number of thunderstorms and days of thunder with and without lightning. Another regular feature recorded the number of wills and the value of the property distributed, with estimates of the total value of property transferred from one generation to the next. There had at one time been a proposal to bring together wills and registration records in Somerset House 'so that the public could have ready access under the same easy regulations to both classes of documents; the one containing proofs of death and heirship, the other containing the authority for transferring property at the death of its possessors to their successors'. Although the proposal had not been adopted, George Graham was sufficiently interested in the data to comment at some length. In the report for 1859 he set out the information in the form of a frequency table for different bands of property values and he also classified the possessors of the various properties according to the census classifications. 'Of 66 persons dying possessed of £100,000 and upwards,' he wrote, 'one was a woman; 10 were peers and titled persons. 37 are described as esquires or gentlemen; but solicitors will be able to say whether these designations are not applied to men who have made large fortunes by trade, commerce and manufactures.'

In the Annual Report for 1873, George Graham included what would today be called a road accident table showing deaths in the streets of London caused by horses and vehicles for the five years 1869–73.

Deaths in the streets of London, caused by horses or vehicles in the five years 1869–73
(*Thirty-sixth Report of the Registrar General, 1873*)

YEARS.	BY HORSES	BY VEHICLES.								DEATHS by HORSES and VEHICLES.
		Carriage.	Omnibus.	Tram-car.	Cab.	Van, Wagon.	Dray.	Cart.	Others.	
1869 - -	10	6	18	—	26	59	3	70	—	192
1870 - -	10	12	20	—	29	63	8	51	5	198
1871 - -	9	12	20	—	23	74	4	60	6	208
1872 - -	8	15	24	—	24	82	7	52	1	213
1873 - -	13	10	12	17	28	75	4	56	2	217
Total 1869-73	50	55	94	17	130	353	26	289	14	1028

DEATHS in the STREETS of LONDON caused by HORSES or VEHICLES in the 5 Years 1869-73.

Rather earlier, in the 16th Annual Report for 1853, he comments on the important use of the indexes prepared by his department 'by means of which the entry of any registered birth, death, or marriage can generally be referred to, on the mere mention of a name, in a very short space of time'. He then goes on to include an entertaining analysis of family nomenclature in England and Wales. After commenting that the English people have an extraordinary number and variety of surnames he chastises the Welsh for their paucity of names, saying that 'John Jones' is a perpetual incognito in Wales, 'and being proclaimed at the cross of the market town would indicate no-one in particular'. He suggests that a partial remedy might be for them to adopt a more extended range of Christian names, if they could be persuaded to depart from ancient customs so far as to forego the use of scriptural and other common names usually given to their children in baptism.

Graham, throughout his years at the GRO, had the support of

The Registrar General analyses family names in the records
(*Sixteenth Report of the Registrar General, 1853*)

In Wales, however, the surnames, if *surnames* they can be called, do not present the same variety, most of them having been formed in a simple manner from the Christian or fore-name of the father in the genitive case, *son* being understood. Thus, Evan's son became **Evans**, John's son **Jones**, &c. Others were derived from the father's name coalesced with a form of the word *ap* or *hab* (son of), by which Hugh ap Howell became **Powell**, Evan ap Hugh became **Pugh**, and in like manner were formed nearly all the Welsh surnames beginning with the letters B and P. Hereditary surnames were not in use even amongst the gentry of Wales until the time of Henry VIII., nor were they generally established until a much later period; indeed, at the present day they can scarcely be said to be adopted amongst the lower classes in the wilder districts, where, as the marriage registers show, the Christian name of the father still frequently becomes the patronymic of the son in the manner just described.

William Farr who was equally concerned about public policies and the general economic and social background to the work they were doing. The various reports of the GRO, though published in the name of the Registrar General, were to a large extent based on Farr's work. Customarily, however, he also addressed his own personal letter to the Registrar General in the appendix to the Annual Reports. Thus, in 1874, he wrote that all the diseases recorded in medical history remain and they have to be kept under constant observation. His remarks, as shown in the extract quoted, are as true today as they were then, over a hundred years ago.

APPENDIX.

LETTER to the REGISTRAR GENERAL on the CAUSES of DEATH in ENGLAND, by W. FARR, Esq., M.D., F.R.S.

YEAR 1874.

SIR,

THE causes of death recur in these ages with great constancy. None of those great plagues which once swept away so many thousands of the people of England have been recently observed. At the same time, in modified forms, all the diseases that have been recorded in medical history remain ; they are not easily stamped out ; they are fatal year after year in certain numbers, and have to be kept under constant observation. The increase of population, the extension of navigation, the new industries, the marvellous chemical operations going on, the explosive forces, the machines, and the power of steam, every year in increased activity, have developed dangers unknown in other days ; and have to be encountered by new remedies. Then nations are now so associated by intercourse that a disease generated among the lowest races in unfavourable conditions may spread to every other race, and carry off many victims.

The opening paragraph of Farr's annual Letter to the Registrar General, on the causes of death in England, 1874
(*Thirty-second Report of the Registrar General, 1874*)

A few years later, after the passing of the Local Government Act in 1871 and the Public Health Act in 1872, Graham commented that a new era may be said to have commenced in the promotion of public health. (See Chapter 9 on health statistics.) A few years later, in 1875, a second Public Health Act was passed. During the rest of the century death rates and infectious disease fell steadily, responding to the improvements in public health and to better housing and other social conditions.

After 1880, when both Farr and Graham had retired from the GRO, the reports prepared by the Registrar General changed and were less concerned with commenting on the economic and social background of the country. The reasons are diverse. In some degree it was perhaps less obvious what particular contribution the

CRO could make to general public debate, and more evident that the work of the Office might best be served by concentrating on the more specialist analyses of fertility and mortality undertaken by Ogle, Tatham and Stevenson who followed Farr as statistical superintendents (see Chapters 10 and 11 on health statistics and on population). A further reason was that other reports, such as that from the Chief Medical Officer, had in the meantime become available. It was also likely that the reports were influenced by the increasing sophistication of the statistics available. As it became easier to present the material in the form of standardised tables, so the reporting itself became more stereotyped.

From time to time, however, the reports included interesting analyses which tried to throw light on changes noted in the statistics. Thus in 1885, when the marriage rate fell to one of its lowest levels and there was increasing interest in changes in fertility, Sir Brydges Hennicker, who succeeded Graham, included in his Annual Report a table setting marriage rates alongside imports, exports, the price of wheat and the value per head of the amount cleared through bankers' clearing house operations. He remarked that previous reports had said that marriages increase as the price of food diminishes, but in his view 'the very opposite has been the case, and the marriage-rate has on the whole varied not inversely but directly with the price of food, or rather of wheat'.

In the second half of the century also, in both the Annual Reports and the *Quarterly Returns*, statistics began to be included from countries overseas and from 'Foreign Cities', together with some comment on the lessons to be learnt from the comparisons.

One of the main changes in the early part of the twentieth century was the introduction of charts as a regular feature in the Annual Reports. For the most part, however, although a number of specific individual reports and papers have been published, particularly by medical statisticians, during the present century until the time of the setting up of OPCS in 1970 the more general reports and publications of the Registrar General include little to suggest or explain changes in the information being collected. Towards the end of the 1960s even the Annual Reports were published without commentary.

The Census Act of 1920, which put census-taking on a permanent basis, required the Registrar General 'from time to time to collect and publish any available statistical information with respect to the number and condition of the population in the interval between one census and another'. The Population Statistics Act in 1938 reaffirmed this duty in its very first section, which put registration in the context of 'the compilation of

TABLE A.—MARRIAGE-RATE, BRITISH EXPORTS and IMPORTS, PRICE of WHEAT, and amount cleared at the London Bankers' Clearing House, 1860–85.*

YEARS.	Marriage-rate.	Value per Head of Population of United Kingdom.			Average Price of Wheat per Quarter.	Amount cleared at the Bankers' Clearing House per Head of Population.
		Exports of British Produce.	Imports.	Total Exports and Imports.		
Cols.	1.	2.	3.	4.	5.	6.
		£ s. d.	£ s. d.	£ s. d.	s. d.	£
1860	17·1	4 11 5	7 6 4	13 0 8	53 3	—
1861	16·3	4 6 4	7 10 1	13 0 3	55 4	—
1862	16·1	4 4 10	7 14 4	13 8 0	55 5	—
1863	16·8	4 19 6	8 8 11	15 2 7	44 8	—
1864	17·2	5 8 1	9 5 3	16 8 7	40 2	—
1865	17·5	5 10 10	9 1 2	16 7 5	41 9	—
1866	17·5	6 5 4	9 15 11	17 14 5	49 11	—
1867	16·5	5 19 0	9 1 0	16 9 6	64 5	—
1868	16·1	5 17 1	9 12 1	17 0 6	63 9	158
1869	15·9	6 2 8	9 10 9	17 3 9	48 2	162
1870	16·1	6 7 8	9 14 1	17 10 3	46 10	174
1871	16·7	7 1 5	10 9 10	19 9 6	56 10	210
1872	17·4	8 0 10	11 2 7	21 0 0	57 1	255
1873	17·6	7 18 7	11 10 10	21 4 2	58 8	264
1874	17·0	7 7 5	11 7 9	20 11 0	55 9	249
1875	16·7	6 16 2	11 7 10	19 19 4	45 2	235
1876	16·5	6 0 11	11 6 1	19 0 10	46 2	203
1877	15·7	5 18 6	11 15 0	19 5 5	56 9	203
1878	15·2	5 13 8	10 17 5	18 2 1	46 5	200
1879	14·4	5 11 9	10 11 9	17 16 10	43 10	195
1880	14·9	6 8 11	11 17 8	20 3 3	44 4	222
1881	15·1	6 14 0	11 7 4	19 17 5	45 4	243
1882	15·5	6 16 10	11 14 0	20 7 8	45 0	236
1883	15·4	6 14 8	11 19 9	20 11 3	41 7	221
1884	15·1	6 9 7	10 16 11	19 1 6	35 8	214
1885	14·4	5 17 3	10 4 3	17 13 7	32 10	200

* The figures in the marriage-rate column are not strictly comparable with those in the value columns, inasmuch as the former relate only to England and Wales, while the latter relate to the whole of the United Kingdom. The figures in the value columns are derived from the Board of Trade Statistical Abstracts. The figures showing the amount cleared at the London Bankers' Clearing House are calculated upon the population of England and Wales, and are also derived from the Board of Trade Statistical Abstracts.

This table was published in 1885, when the marriage rate had fallen to a very low level. The Registrar General at the time remarked that 'the marriage rate has on the whole varied . . . directly with the price of food, or rather of wheat'.
(*Forty-eighth Report of the Registrar General, 1885*)

statistical information with respect to the social and civil condition of the populations of Great Britain'. That Sir Sylvanus Vivian, who held the post of Registrar General from 1921 to 1945, did not attempt to report on social changes in the way that his predecessors did in the early years of the GRO, reflects changed attitudes towards Government and the less conspicuous role which the GRO itself expected to play.

The situation today is very different. It is the result of political change, emanating from the growth of the welfare state and the need to collect much more information about what is happening to people, and a major change affecting the GRO itself. In 1970 it was merged with the Government Social Survey to form the Office of Population Censuses and Surveys (see Chapter 8 on social surveys) and, in 1972, a professional statistician, George Payne, was appointed Registrar General with the rank of Deputy Secretary. These changes shifted the emphasis away from the administration of registration and more towards the uses of the data which could be derived from it and from the Census of Population and other surveys. They followed a major reconstruction of the Government Statistical Service under Professor, later Sir Claus, Moser which at the same time led to more emphasis being put on social statistics. 1970 also saw the publication by the Central Statistical Office of the annual *Social Trends* which drew heavily on material held by OPCS and on the advice of its statisticians. It is interesting to speculate whether, had previous Registrars General taken the opportunity to publish regular social reports, the initiative for the publication might have come from OPCS rather than the CSO.

The establishment of OPCS, and the integration within it of social surveys opened up the possibility of a whole new range of statistics, some of which are discussed in Chapter 8 on social surveys. One of the first of these new sources, the General Household Survey, led to a regular series of reports on social conditions. Moreover there is now a sustained flow of comment from other publications, such as *Population Trends*, the regular publications on different aspects of mortality and morbidity, and the series of Monitors designed to provide early publication of certain statistics on some of OPCS's work. There is no annual report covering the work of OPCS as a whole but there is instead a series of annual reviews covering all the special subjects with which the Office is concerned. A detailed list of publications currently available is contained in Appendix C.

The population controversy and the first population census

Early history

Under the Population Act, 1840, the Registrar General was made responsible for the Census of Population for England and Wales and the first census carried out by him was in 1841. There had already been four earlier censuses in 1801, 1811, 1821 and 1831.

Census-taking has a long history[1,2]. The Babylonians, the Egyptians and the Chinese all collected statistics about their people, mainly for military and taxation purposes, but also, as in Egypt, for other purposes such as planning the building of the Pyramids and sharing out the land after the annual flooding of the Nile. In the millennium before Christ the Greeks and Romans were also conducting censuses. The Roman census, carried out every five years, required each man to return to his place of origin and it was the census ordered by Caesar Augustus which brought Joseph and Mary to Bethlehem when Jesus was born. The Hebrews themselves had also carried out censuses, the most notorious being that by King David. It was interrupted by plague and never completed, and so led to the belief that census-taking

Biblical references to census-taking
St Luke, Chapter 2

And it came to pass in those days, that there went out a decree from Cæsar Augustus, that all the world should be taxed.
2(*And* this taxing was first made when Cȳ-rē-nĭ-ŭs was governor of Syria.)
3 And all went to be taxed, every one into his own city.
4And Joseph also went up from Galilee, out of the city of Nazareth, into Judæa, unto the city of David, which is called Bethlehem; (because he was of the house and lineage of David:)
5To be taxed with Mary his espoused wife, being great with child.

2 Samuel, Chapter 24

1 And again the anger of the Lord was kindled against Israel, and he moved David against them to say, Go, number Israel and Judah.
2 For the King said to Jō-ăb the captain of the host, which *was* with him, Go now through all the tribes of Israel, from Dan even to Beersheba, and number ye the people, that I may know the number of the people.
9 And Jō-ăb gave up the sum of the number of the people unto the king: and there were in Israel eight hundred thousand valiant men that drew the sword; and the men of Judah *were* five hundred thousand men.
10¶ And David's heart smote him after that he had numbered the people. And David said unto the LORD, I have sinned greatly in that I have done: and now, I beseech thee, O LORD, take away the iniquity of thy servant; for I have done very foolishly.

was a dangerous practice likely to incur the wrath of God.

In England and Wales the first major enumeration took place in 1066, under William I. The results, set out in the Domesday Book, contained a detailed inventory of land and property. In Elizabeth's reign, in the second half of the sixteenth century, bishops were asked to count the number of families in their diocese and report back to the Privy Council; a similar exercise was carried out by James I in the first half of the seventeenth century. Regular population censuses were not carried out until the beginning of the nineteenth century.

Elsewhere, by this time, censuses were already well established. Quebec had completed one as early as 1666. Iceland undertook one in 1703 and Sweden in 1749, and in the middle of the eighteenth century censuses were also taken in Germany and other European states. In the United States religious opposition delayed census-taking until 1790 because God-fearing churchgoers recalled what befell the Israelites in the time of King David and thus regarded counting people as sacrilegious.

The 1753 Census Bill and the Malthus controversy

Similar attitudes also prevailed in England and Wales. A Bill, which Mr Thomas Potter, MP for St Germans in Cornwall, introduced into the House of Commons in 1753, to carry out an annual census and to institute registration of births, marriages and deaths provoked a speech from Mr Matthew Ridley, MP for Newcastle upon Tyne, saying that his constituents 'looked upon the proposal as ominous, and feared lest some great public misfortune or an epidemical distemper should follow the numbering'. The main opposition, however, came from those who feared that the results might disclose to foreign enemies the weakness of the country or that it would impair the liberty of the individual – a 'most effectual engine of rapacity and oppression' – as it was described by Mr Thornton, the member for York. Although the Bill was carried by a large majority in the House of Commons, it was defeated in the Lords[3].

The Bill was introduced at a time when there was considerable debate about the size of the population and some concern that it might be declining. For example, the Rev Richard Price, a well-known Nonconformist minister who was also greatly interested in insurance and annuities, held that the population was about five million and had declined dramatically since the 'Glorious Revolution of 1688'. In his important and influential book, published in 1780 and known as *Dr Price's Reversionary*

Payments, he expressed concern about the possibility that, 'amidst all our splendours, we are decreasing so fast, as to have lost, in about 70 years, near a quarter of our people'. The full title of Dr Price's book, which went into many editions, is given below.

> Observations on Reversionary Payments; on Schemes for providing Annuities for Widows, and Persons in Old Age; on the Method of Calculating the Values of Assurance on Lives; and on the National Debt, also Essays on different Subjects in the Doctrine of Life Annuities and Political Arithmetic; a Collection of New Tables, and a Postcript on the Population of the Kingdom.

Various other people had been making estimates of the size of the population using indicators such as the amount of bread consumed or the number of houses multiplied by an assumed number of persons per house. Gregory King, a genealogist and engraver best known as a statistician, made the first systematic attempt in 1695, when he estimated the number of houses in England and Wales as 1.3 million and the number of people as 5.5 million. The Rev Price's calculations were derived mainly from the number of houses estimated from the Hearth Tax and the Window Tax returns and from samples of baptisms and burials in parish registers. He had also noticed the half-empty churches and the decay and disappearance of many houses. He linked this apparent depopulation with the burden of the national debt, with 'the increasing burthens which oppressed the poor' and also to the growth of great towns which 'become checks on population of too hurtful a nature, nurseries of debauchery and voluptuousness; and in many respects, greater evils than can be compensated by any advantages'[5].

Towards the end of the century others, such as the Rev John Howlett, a Church of England parson, took the opposite view and maintained that numbers were steadily rising. The Hearth and the Window Tax returns were used for many of the estimates but, as these taxes were not imposed on poor households and in any case were often not very reliable, the resulting population estimates were subject to wide margins of error. Recent research suggests that there was indeed a small decline in numbers in England and Wales from 5.3 million in 1656 to 4.9 million in 1686 but that by 1716 the numbers had recovered and had reached 5.8 million by 1750 (Chart 5.1)[6].

During the rest of the century it was becoming clear that the population was increasing and the controversy was fuelled by the publication, in 1798, of Thomas Robert Malthus's *Essay on the Principle of Population*. Malthus, who was born in 1766 and died in 1834, was Professor of Political Economy and Modern History at

Chart 5.1   Population change,
England, 1541–1871
(Source: Wrigley and Schofield[6])

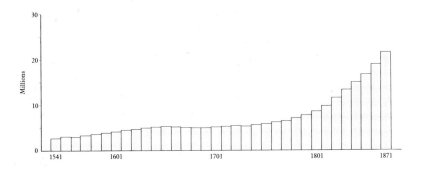

the East India Company's college at Haileybury. Although he also made an important contribution to the development of economic thought, he is mainly remembered for his theory on population which had a profound and lasting influence on political and economic thinking throughout the nineteenth century. This sought to reduce population variations to the simple principle that, whereas food supplies rarely increase faster than in arithmetic progression, population tends to increase in geometric progression:

> That population cannot increase without the means of subsistence, is a proposition so evident, that it needs no illustration.
> That population does invariably increase, where there are the means of subsistence, the history of every people that have ever existed will abundantly prove.
> And that the superior power cannot be checked, without producing misery or vice, the ample portion of these two bitter ingredients in the cup of human life, and the continuance of the physical causes that seem to have produced them, bear too convincing a testimony. (Malthus. *Population*. 1798.)

In practice, according to Malthus, both positive and preventive checks occur. The positive check works through increased mortality arising from famine and disease and the preventive check through fewer births. Only by late marriage, and hence small families, could a properly Christian society avoid both the misery of poverty and disease through over-population. Malthus regarded the preventive check of physical contraception as abhorrent and a vice.

The first edition of Malthus's essay ran to only 50,000 words, but by the sixth edition, in 1826, it had been expanded to no less than 225,000 words and translations were appearing in many languages. His theory was not original: the problem he posed was already familiar to Plato and Aristotle and, in England itself shortly before Malthus, David Hume and others had been putting forward similar views. The significance of his work is that it reminded the social reformers of the time, such as William Godwin and even Karl Marx, that their plans for Utopia could be brought to nothing because of a systematic demographic flaw. It was this aspect of his work which generated strong emotions and led to so much controversy. His firmly held belief in his population theory led Malthus himself to campaign for the reform of the English Poor Laws, particularly what had become known as the Speenhamland system whereby payments were made to the families of destitute people. This, Malthus believed, only encouraged early marriage and hence more births.

The need to know exactly what was happening led him, and others who were also concerned about the effect on the population of emigration and colonisation, to press for a census to be undertaken:

> For thirty years the country has ceased to export (food) and has become dependent upon its neighbours, so that it is necessary to ascertain whether this is due mainly to increase of population and, if so, how far agriculture must be extended . . . .

The Census Act, 1800

The population controversy and a succession of bad harvests at the end of the eighteenth century helped to make sure that when a second Census Bill came before Paliament in 1800 it had an easy passage: it was presented on 20 November by Mr Abbot, member for Helston in Cornwall, passed on 3 December, and received the Royal Assent on 31 December. The whole census operation was

41° GEORGII III. Cap. 15.

Extract from the first Census Act in 1800

II.

FORM of the PRECEPT for giving Notice to High Conftables, Overfeers, and Houfeholders, in *England*, of the Time and Place appointed by Juftices of the Peace for taking the Anfwers and Returns under this Act.

———————

The County, &c. to wit. } *To the Conftable,* [*Tythingman, or Headborough*] *of in the faid County.*

YOU are hereby required, with all convenient Speed, to give or caufe to be given Notice to the High Conftable of the Hundred of and to the Overfeers of the Poor of every Parifh, Townfhip, or Place, within the faid Hundred; and if there is no Overfeer therein, then to fome fubftantial Houfeholder therein; that they are feverally required to appear at completed in a remarkably short time. Enumeration took place on Monday, 10 March 1801 and the first abstracts were printed on 21 December of that year. John Rickman, who was previously a clerk in the House of Commons and had been closely involved in the preparation of the Census Bill, prepared the abstracts and reports not only for this Census but for the three succeeding ones: he described himself as 'appointed by His Majesty's Most Honorable Privy Council to digest and reduce into Order the above Abstract'[7]. His results gave a total population for England and Wales of about 9 million, the previous estimates having varied from between 8 to 11 million.

The individuals chosen to act as enumerators in England and Wales, who made house-to-house enquiries, were the Overseers of the Poor or, failing them, substantial householders assisted by church officials and, if need be, 'constables, tithingmen, headboroughs or other peace officers.' The Act also applied to Scotland where the responsibility was placed on schoolmasters. The local returns, which were statistical summaries unsupported by names and addresses, had to be made in a prescribed form and attested before the Justices of the Peace. Payment was made to the officials and their expenses were met.

The Census was divided into two parts. The first, carried out by the enumerators, was concerned with finding out the number of people (males and females separately), families and houses (both inhabited and uninhabited) and with obtaining information about individual occupations in three groups – agriculture; trade, manufacture or handicraft; and others. It is interesting to note that the replies to the question on employment were not properly understood. In some cases women, children and servants were classed with the householder and in other cases they were included in the third category as being in neither agricultural nor commercial occupations. The family at the time of the Census still regarded itself as an economic unit and the concept of an individual with his or her own occupation separate from the family was unfamiliar[8] (see Chapter 6).

The second part of the Census was concerned with whether the population was increasing or decreasing. The clergy were asked to give details from their records of baptisms and burials over the years 1700–1801 and the number of marriages in each year from 1754 to 1800, 1754 being the first year under the 1753 Marriage Act, in which all marriages had to be registered. At subsequent censuses, up to and including 1841, the clergy had to make similar returns for the preceding decade.

Although there were variations from census to census, the

SCHEDULE.

———◆———

I.

QUESTIONS to which, by Directions of an Act paſſed in the Forty-firſt Year of the Reign of His Majeſty King *George* the Third, intituled, *An Act for taking an Account of the Population of* Great Britain, *and of the Increaſe or Diminution thereof*, written Anſwers are to be returned by the Rector, Vicar, Curate, or Officiating Miniſter, and Overſeers of the Poor, or (in Default thereof) by ſome other ſub-ſtantial Houſeholder, of every Pariſh, Townſhip, and Place (including thoſe Places alſo which are Extra-parochial) in *England*; and by the Schoolmaſters or other Perſons to be appointed under the ſaid Act for every Pariſh in *Scotland*; ſigned by them reſpectively, and atteſted upon Oath or Affirmation by the ſaid Overſeers, or (in Default thereof) by ſuch other ſubſtantial Houſeholders as aforeſaid, in *England*, and by the Schoolmaſters or other ſuch Perſons as aforeſaid in *Scotland*; for which Purpoſe they are to attend the Juſtices of the Peace, within their reſpective Juriſdictions, at ſuch Times and Places as the ſaid Juſtices of the Peace ſhall appoint, on Pain of incurring the Penalties impoſed by the ſaid Act for every wilful Default or Neglect.

1ſt. How many Inhabited Houſes are there in your Pariſh, Town-ſhip, or Place; by how many Families are they occupied; and, how many Houſes therein are Uninhabited?

2d. How many Perſons (including Children of whatever Age) are there actually found within the Limits of your Pariſh, Town-ſhip, or Place, at the Time of taking this Account, diſtin-guiſhing Males and Females, and excluſive of Men actually ſerving in His Majeſty's Regular Forces or Militia, and excluſive of Seamen either in His Majeſty's Service, or be-longing to Regiſtered Veſſels?

3d. What Number of Perſons, in your Pariſh, Townſhip, or Place, are chiefly employed in Agriculture; how many in Trade, Manufactures, or Handicraft; and, how many are not com-prized in any of the preceding Claſſes?

4th. What was the Number of Baptiſms and Burials in your Pariſh, Townſhip, or Place, in the ſeveral Years 1700, 1710, 1720, 1730, 1740, 1750, 1760, 1770, 1780, and each ſubſequent Year to the 31ſt Day of *December* 1800, diſtinguiſhing Males from Females?

5th. What has been the Number of Marriages in your Pariſh, Townſhip, or Place, in each Year, from the Year 1754 incluſive to the End of the Year 1800?

6th. Are there any Matters which you think it neceſſary to re-mark in Explanation of your Anſwers to any of the pre-ceding Queſtions?

The 1801 Census of Population schedule

FORM of ANSWERS by the CLERGYMEN in ENGLAND,

To the Questions contained in the Schedule to an Act, intituled, *An Act for taking an Account of the Population of* Great Britain, *and of the Increase or Diminution thereof.*

County, &c.	Hundred, &c.	City, Town, &c.	Parish, &c.
Bedfordshire	Bedford	Bedford	St. Paul's

QUESTION 4th.

Years.	BAPTISMS.		BURIALS.		Years.	BAPTISMS.		BURIALS.	
	Males.	Females.	Males.	Females.		Males.	Females.	Males.	Females.
1700	24	25	19	16	1787	23	29	44	38
1710	15	26	34	27	1788	30	21	21	27
1720	24	22	20	21	1789	31	28	21	44
1730	27	24	26	27	1790	26	35	20	22
1740	19	17	35	23	1791	22	28	42	38
1750	14	12	13	15	1792	21	27	28	42
1760	19	28	11	15	1793	27	21	31	50
1770	33	24	28	36	1794	23	36	42	45
1780	20	21	27	33	1795	16	31	23	43
1781	25	25	43	28	1796	25	23	32	30
1782	35	16	41	42	1797	24	18	28	27
1783	29	30	35	35	1798	28	29	27	29
1784	27	21	25	33	1799	24	22	21	31
1785	30	28	34	34	1800	33	43	26	30
1786	28	27	38	29					

QUESTION 5th.

MARRIAGES.

Years.	Number of Marriages.	Years.	Number of Marriages.	Years.	Number of Marriages.	Years.	Number of Marriages.
1754	16	1766	29	1778	22	1790	25
1755	19	1767	22	1779	27	1791	24
1756	12	1768	25	1780	27	1792	21
1757	16	1769	26	1781	38	1793	33
1758	10	1770	23	1782	13	1794	21
1759	22	1771	23	1783	22	1795	24
1760	28	1772	17	1784	16	1796	38
1761	24	1773	22	1785	35	1797	24
1762	27	1774	17	1786	17	1798	31
1763	21	1775	13	1787	23	1799	24
1764	18	1776	21	1788	31	1800	24
1765	13	1777	23	1789	28		

REMARKS, (if any) in Explanation of the Matters stated in Answer to the 4th and 5th Questions.

4th Question. *If the Burials much exceed the Baptisms, it may be accounted for from the great Number of Dissenters in this Parish, where Children are monthly baptized in their Meetings.*

5th Question.

CERTIFICATE OF THE CLERGYMAN.

I, *John Mansted* [Rector, Vicar, Curate, or officiating Minister,] of the Parish, Township, &c. of *St. Paul's Bedford* in the County of *Bedford* do certify, That the above Return contains, to the best of my Knowledge and Belief, a full and true Answer to the 4th and 5th Questions contained in the Schedule to an Act, intituled, *An Act for taking an Account of the Population of* Great Britain, *and of the Increase or Diminution thereof.*

Witness *E. Palmer* One of the Overseers [or substantial Householders] of the said Parish, &c. of *St. Paul's* this *16th* Day of *April 1801.*

FORM of ANSWERS by the OVERSEERS, &c. in ENGLAND,

To the Questions contained in the Schedule to an Act, intituled, *An Act for taking an Account of the Population of* Great Britain, *and of the Increase or Diminution thereof.*

County, &c.	Hundred, &c.	City, Town, &c.	Parish, &c.	QUESTION 1st. HOUSES.			QUESTION 2d. PERSONS, including Children of whatever Age.		Total of PERSONS in Answer to Question 2d.	QUESTION 3d. OCCUPATIONS.			TOTAL of PERSONS. N. B. This Column must correspond with the Total of Persons in Answer to Question 2d.
				Inhabited.	By how many Families occupied.	Uninhabited.	Males.	Females.		Persons chiefly employed in Agriculture.	Persons chiefly employed in Trade, Manufactures, or Handicraft.	All other Persons not comprised in the Two preceding Classes.	
Bedford	Barford	— — —	Eatonbray	339	461	12	737	888	1625	189	117	1319	1625

N. B. *If any Family occupies Two or more Houses in different Parishes, Townships, or Places, the Individuals belonging to such Family are to be numbered only in those Parishes, Townships, or Places where they severally happen to be at the Time of taking the Account.*

Above, a completed clergyman's schedule in the Census of 1801. The clergyman's remark reads 'if the burials much exceed the Baptisms it may be accounted from the Great Number of Difsenters in this Parish, where Childen are monthly baptised in their meetings'. Below, an Overseer's schedule

1801 model continued generally to be applied for the next three censuses. There were, however, various changes in content. In 1811 a distinction was made between houses being built and those uninhabited for other reasons, such as dilapidation, and – as a consequence of the problems experienced in the first census – information was collected about families engaged in occupations instead of people. In 1821 there was a first attempt to analyse population by age. This was important for a number of purposes, but particularly at this time because of the growing demand for accurate life tables from Friendly Societies and others concerned with actuarial matters: such tables cannot be prepared without reference to the age structure of the total population. Enumerators were given discretion to record statements of age in five-year groups, and in about eight out of nine cases they were able to do so[9]:

> If you are of the Opinion that in making the preceding Enquiries . . . the Ages of the several individuals can be obtained in a manner satisfactory to yourself, and not inconvenient to the Parties, be pleased to state . . . the Number of those who are under 5 Years of Age, of those between 5 and 10 Years of Age . . . distinguishing Males from Females. (*Guide to Census Reports, Great Britain 1801–1966*)

The question was not repeated in the 1831 Census, presumably because Rickman considered that once the age distribution had been determined from the 1821 Census there was no need to update it. The 1831 Census, however, sought greater details about the occupations of the male population aged twenty and over. Because this Census required enumerators to collect fuller information than on previous occasions, more instructions and special sheets were issued to help them.

For their assistance herein a prepared Formula (*No. 1.*) *is transmitted with every Schedule, such as may be used in* "*proceeding from House to House on the 30th Day of May next, and on the Days immediately subsequent thereto, if one day shall not be sufficient,*" *and by means of this Formula the account will be readily taken (in hard black-lead pencil or ink) by marks across the several Lines, thus :* —

//

such account to be summed together afterwards for insertion in the Schedule, by dividing it into Tens *for counting, thus :*

// = 43

Example of the special sheets issued in 1831 to help census enumerators collect a wider range of information

John Rickman, who had done so much to establish the censuses and who prepared the first abstracts or reports, died in 1840 shortly after the GRO was set up and before the 1841 Census was carried out. He was no dull statistician and, in tribute to him, this chapter concludes with an extract from the words of praise written about him in a letter on 3 November 1800, from his friend Charles Lamb to Thomas Manning.

This Rickman lived in our Buildings, immediately opposite our house; the finest fellow to drop in a'nights, about nine or ten o'clock – cold bread and cheese time – just in the wishing time of the night, when you wish for somebody to come in, without a distinct idea of the probable anybody. Just in the nick, neither too early to be tedious, not too late to sit a reasonable time. He is a most pleasant hand: a fine rattling fellow, has gone through life laughing at solemn apes – himself hugely literate, oppressively full of information in all stuff of conversation, from matter of fact to Xenophon and Plato – can talk Greek with Porson, politics with Thelwall, conjecture with George Dyer, nonsense with me, and anything with anybody; great farmer, somewhat concerned in an agricultural magazine; reads no poetry but Shakespeare; very intimate with Southey, but never reads his poetry; relishes George Dyer; thoroughly penetrates into the ridiculous wherever found; understands the first time (a great desideratum in common minds) – you never need speak twice to him; does not want explanations, translations, limitations; as Professor Godwin does when you make an assertion; is up to anything, down to anything; whatever sapit hominum! A perfect man![10]

References

1. OPCS. *Teachers' Notes for the Census; History in the Census.* 1981, London, OPCS.

2. S P Vivian, Registrar General. *The History of the Census.* 1923, unpublished lecture delivered at the GRO.

3. Registrar General. *The Story of the General Register Office and its Origins from 1536 to 1937.* 1937, London, HMSO.

4. Patricia James. *Population Malthus: his Life and Times.* 1979, London, RKP.

5. D V Glass. *Numbering the People.* 1973, Farnborough, Saxon House.

6. E A Wrigley and R S Schofield, *The Population History of England, 1571–1871.* 1981, London, Arnold.

7. Glass. Op. cit.

8. OPCS. *Guide to Census Reports, Great Britain, 1801–1966.* 1977, London, HMSO.

9. Glass. Op. cit.

10. Registrar General. *The Story of the General Register Office and its Origins from 1536 to 1937.* 1937, London, HMSO.

The census: the first 100 years of the General Register Office

The censuses of 1841 and 1851

In addition to the new system of registration of birth, marriages and deaths which led to the setting up of the GRO in 1837, the Registrar General was also, by the Population Act 1840, given responsibility for the Census of Population in England and Wales. Thomas Lister's correspondence with the Counsel employed by the Government to prepare the Bill demonstrates once again the care and thoroughness with which he planned the undertaking. No longer were the Overseers of the Poor to be the responsible enumerators but the administration was to be based on the local machinery of the new registration service. Lister was quick to appreciate that the bringing together of these two basic sets of information would make it possible for the first time to collect material on a national scale in a uniform and systematic way.

The first aim in remodelling the enumeration methods for the Census of Population in 1841 was to make sure that there were no omissions or double-counting of heads. This meant taking the census everywhere at the same time and in the shortest possible time. England and Wales was already divided into 2,193 registration districts and, for the purpose of the census, each was sub-divided into an appropriate number of enumeration districts ranging from not more than 200 to not less than 25 inhabited houses. A trial run, or pilot survey as it would now be called, was held in various different types of district to find out how many households an enumerator could cover in one day, and 35,000 enumerators were consequently appointed. An excerpt from the detailed instructions sent by the Registrar General to the registrars on how to decide on the size of enumeration districts is shown in the illustration on page 59. The letter book in which these hand-copied records were kept is a fine example of the clarity of thought and easy flowing style of Thomas Lister and a reminder of his literary talents as a novelist as well as his administrative abilities as Registrar General.

The 1841 Census has been called the first 'modern' census because it broke with the tradition established by John Rickman whereby returns were usually recorded locally in summary form only and then sent in digested form to London. Instead a separate

schedule was provided for each householder and the names and characteristics of every individual in the household were listed. The full returns were then sent to London for analysis at the GRO[1].

This new procedure was carried out by delivering self-completion forms to each household a few days before the appointed day of the census. The householder had to fill in the form in respect of all persons sleeping in the house on Sunday, 6th June, before the arrival of the enumerator on the following day; penalties could be imposed for failing to do this. The enumerator had to ensure that as far as possible the schedule was complete and correct, and he then had to transfer the answers to his own schedule. Once again the instructions from the Registrar General set out in detail how this was to be done, including a note saying that 'A sufficient number of black lead pencils will be sent to the Registrar, of which he must give one to each Enumerator, to be

Opposite, Census-taking in 1861; a cartoon from the *Illustrated News*, 13 April 1861

"You must divide the District of which you are Registrar into "districts for Enumeration, each of which shall contain not more "than 200 inhabited houses and not less than 25 – In so doing "you must consider the distance to be traversed by the –– "Enumerator in going from house to house, and must so form "the districts as to comprise more houses when they lie near "together, as in a Town, and fewer where they lie far apart

"Thus, in a Town where the houses touch each other, or a "only a few yards apart, the number included in the Enume-"ration district may be from 130 to 200 inhabited houses; "in a Town or Village where they are still near though –– "farther apart than in a closely built Town, the number "may be from 80 to 130; in a scattered Village or rural "district in which there is occasionally a distance of more than "half a mile between one house and the next nearest, the "number included may be from 50 to 80; and it is only where "the population is thinly scattered over the country and –– "intervals of two miles and upwards intervene between some "of the houses and others which are nearest to them, that –– "the district may include less than 50 inhabited houses"

"With reference to the thinly-inhabited districts, it is to "be observed, that in no case must the district include a "larger extent of country than an able-bodied and active "man, visiting every house therein, can go over between –– "sunrise and sunset in a summer's day".

The Registrar General instructs registrars on how to determine the size of enumeration districts, for the 1841 Census
(From *History of Census 1841*)

A specimen of an enumerator's schedule in the 1841 Census of Population
(*Census 1841: Enumeration Abstract*)

SPECIMEN OF ENUMERATOR'S SCHEDULE.

(TITLE PAGE.)

County of_____ (*Parliamentary Division*)_____

Hundred, Wapentake, Soke, or Liberty of _____

Parish of _____

Township of _____

City, or Borough, or Town, or County Corporate of _____

Within the Limits of the Parliamentary Boundary of the City or Borough of _____

Within the Municipal Boundary of _____

_____

Superintendent Registrar's District _____

Registrar's District _____

No. of Enumeration District _____

Description of ditto _____

[*Here follow a sufficient number of lines to insert the description of the District.*]

_____

[*Specimen page, showing how Entries were made.*]

City or Borough of *Southwark.*
Parish or Township of *St. Saviour.*

{*Example of Enumeration Schedule,*
{*showing how Entries may be made.*}

PLACE.	HOUSES.		Names of each Person who abode therein the preceding Night.	Age and Sex.		Profession, Trade, Employment, or of Independent Means.	Where Born.	
	Uninhabited or Building.	Inhabited.		Males.	Females.		Whether Born in same County.	Whether Born in Scotland, Ireland, or Foreign Parts.
George Street – –		1	*James Johnson*	40		*Chemist*	Y.	
			Jane ditto		35		N.	
			William ditto	15		*Shoem. Ap.*	Y.	
			Anne ditto		13		Y.	
			Edward Smith	30		*Chemist's Sh.*	N.	
			Sarah Robins		45	*F. S.*		*I.*
Do. – – – –	1 U	1	*John Cox*	60		*Publican*	N.	
Do. – – – –	1 B		*Mary ditto*		45		Y.	
Do. – – – –	1 B		*Ellen ditto*		20		N.	
			James Macpherson	25		*M. S.*		*S.*
			Henry Wilson	35		*Army*	N.	
			n. k.	above 20				
Extra-Parochial Place, named "The Close."		1	*William Jones*	50		*Farmer*	Y.	
			Elizabeth ditto		40		Y.	
			William ditto	15		*Navy*	Y.	
			Charlotte ditto		8		Y.	
			n. k. ditto		5 months.		Y.	

Each schedule contained a sufficient number of these pages to embrace the census of the district, each page containing 25 lines.

Directions given as to the Manner in which Entries were to be made in the Enumeration Schedule.

After " *City or Borough of*" write the name, if the district is in a city or borough ; if not, draw a line through those words, or through whichever of the two the district does not belong to. After " *Parish or Township of*" write the name ; if there is no township in the parish draw a line through " *Township ;*" if it is a township, write the name of the township, and draw a line through " *Parish.*" If it is extra-parochial draw a line through " *Parish or Township of,*" and write " *Extra-Parochial*" over those words, and after it the name.

used by him in taking an account of the Population of his District, when going from House to House'. The information he had to copy was not as simple as formerly since account now had to be taken of each person individually and details had to be entered in the appropriate column opposite each person's name instead of, as previously, merely entering numbers in each household. The details asked for were also more comprehensive. In addition to name, sex, age and occupation, householders were asked to state which persons were foreigners, and which were born in the parish or county in which they were living. Although the schedule may seem simple by today's standards, at that time when there was no universal system of education and large numbers of people were unable to read or write, it is remarkable that householders, even with the help of the enumerators, were able to answer the questions.

The system adopted in 1841 has stood the test of time and has remained more or less unaltered to the present day. Such changes as there have been relate mainly to the methods of processing data. The first of these did not take place until seventy years later, in 1911, when punch-card and mechanical sorting enabled machines instead of clerks to process the data. The next major development had to wait another fifty years, until 1961, when computers were first used to process the punched cards. It is difficult to imagine today what a tremendous feat it must have been for the GRO to process the nineteenth century censuses, with hundreds of clerks carefully tabulating with pen and pencil on large sheets of paper details for every individual in the country.

The Census of Population for 1851 coincided with the year of the Great Exhibition when the country proudly displayed its industrial and technological predominance. The schedule was substantially expanded but thereafter remained very much the same until 1911, with the basic questions consisting of the names of members of households living at specified addresses, their relationship to the head of the household, marital status, age, sex, occupation, birthplace and infirmity. New questions were progressively introduced but their number was limited for fear of making the form too complex.

The 1851 Census was the first to ask questions about marital status and relationship to head of household. Exact age was also to be stated instead of the nearest five-year age-group. One of the most important developments, reflecting the growing diversity of the economy, was the much greater detail required on occupations. A start had already been made in the 1831 and 1841 Censuses, but the extra questions included in 1851 enabled occupations to be

Filling up the census paper.
Wife of his bosom 'Upon my word. Mr
Peewitt! Is this the way you fill up your
census? So you call yourself the "Head
of the Family"—do you—and me a
"female"?' (*Punch* vol XX, 1851)

FILLING UP THE CENSUS PAPER.

Wife of his Bosom. "Upon my word, Mr. Peewitt! Is this the Way you Fill up your Census
So you call Yourself the 'Head of the Family'—do you—and me a 'Female!'"

classified into 'classes' and 'sub-classes'. For the first time, too,
masters in trade and manufacture were asked to put on the
schedule 'master' after the description of their occupation and to
add the number of men they employed on the day of the census.
The form of classification adopted was the first scientific attempt to
classify occupations in any detail and it was to have long-lasting
implications for statistical analysis. In spite of continual modifica-
tion and almost complete revision at later censuses, it remained
basically the same until 1921.

A major development in the 1851 Census was the way
William Farr used the information to classify people by occupation
and age. The analysis, which covered 332 occupations by five-year
age-groups, was an enormous task and was achieved by using work
sheets measuring 26 inches by 40 inches. This information was
particularly important because, in conjunction with deaths registration, it made possible detailed study of occupational mortality.
This linking of two major data sources within the GRO enabled
Farr 'to compare the living in each well defined occupation with
the number dying registered at the corresponding ages; and thus to
determine the influence of employment on health and life'. Among
his conclusions he noted that:

> Miners die in undue proportions, particularly at the advanced ages, when
> their strength begins to decline ... Tailors die in considerable numbers at

the younger ages (25–45) . . . (Labourers') mortality is at nearly the same rate as that of the whole population, except in the very advanced ages, when the Poor Law apparently affords inadequate relief to the worn-out workman.

In 1851 there was a fundamental change in the way the census results were presented. For the first time the Registrar General's commentary was accompanied by two substantial volumes of tables containing data for subdivisions of England and Wales based on a grouping related to districts and sub-districts of the eleven registration divisions already devised for the statistical material in the Annual Reports. The tables were also accompanied by maps depicting the density of population and the distribution of people by occupation.

Associated with the 1851 Census were two important enquiries into religion and education. Plans had been made on the assumption that they could be included as part of the Census, but the House of Lords raised objections to the penalties which could be imposed on people withholding information, and their view was upheld by the legal advisers to the Crown. The Registrar General therefore decided to go ahead on a voluntary basis and people were told that answers to the questions on the special forms were not compulsory. In the event there were few refusals. It is interesting to note that the compulsory status of the population census today similarly inhibits including questions which people might be diffident to answer: for example, a question on income was considered in the original proposals for the 1971 Census, but because of the sensitivity, and complexity, of the question it was not included and was instead the subject of a follow-up survey linked to the census but carried out on a voluntary basis a year later.

The purpose of the religious enquiry was to find out how far the means of instruction provided in Great Britain during the last fifty years had kept pace with the population during the same period, and to what extent those means were adequate 'to meet the spiritual wants of the increased population of 1851'. It was thus primarily concerned with the number and capacity of churches, chapels or rooms regularly used as places of worship and the number of services and attendances at these places. It was published in 1851, and as many as 21,000 copies were sold. According to the author, Horace Mann, a twenty-eight year old barrister who was assistant commissioner for the population census, the most important finding was 'unquestionably, the alarming number of non-attendants'. The report also showed that Protestant Dissenters provided nearly half the church accommodation and that some 45 per cent of those attending services were Protestant Dissenters. There was considerable controversy about the reliability of these results but not surprisingly, although the purpose of the enquiry 'had been to look at provision of facilities rather than numbers of adherents to different sects', they were used by Nonconformists to press their case for disestablishment of the Church of England and the Church in Wales[2].

The religious enquiry in the 1851 Census finds that the labouring classes fail to attend religious services
(*1851 Census Report: Religious Worship, England and Wales*)

> The most important fact which this investigation as to attendance brings before us is, unquestionably, the alarming number of the non-attendants. Even in the least unfavorable aspect of the figures just presented, and assuming (as no doubt is right) that the 5,288,294 absent every Sunday are not always the same individuals, it must be apparent that a sadly formidable portion of the English people are habitual neglecters of the public ordinances of religion. Nor is it difficult to indicate to what particular class of the community this portion in the main belongs. The middle classes have augmented rather than diminished that devotional sentiment and strictness of attention to religious services by which, for several centuries, they have so eminently been distinguished. With the upper classes, too, the subject of religion has obtained of late a marked degree of notice, and a regular church-attendance is now ranked amongst the recognized proprieties of life. It is to satisfy the wants of these two classes that the number of religious structures has of late years so increased. But while the *labouring* myriads of our country have been multiplying with our multiplied material prosperity, it cannot, it is feared, be stated that a corresponding increase has occurred in the attendance of this class in our religious edifices. More especially in cities and large towns it is observable how absolutely insignificant a portion of the congregations is composed of artizans. They fill, perhaps, in youth, our National, British, and Sunday Schools, and there receive the elements of a religious education; but, no sooner do they mingle in the active world of labour than, subjected to the constant action of opposing influences, they soon become as utter strangers to religious ordinances as the people of a heathen country.

Below and opposite, church-going in 1851
(WSF Pickering, The 1851 religious census – a useless experiment? in *The British Journal of Sociology*, 1967)

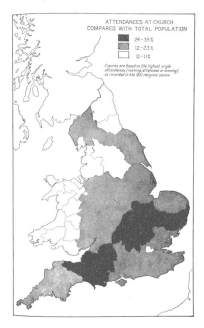

ATTENDANCES AT CHURCH COMPARED WITH TOTAL POPULATION

24-35%
12-23%
0-11%

Figures are based on the highest single attendances (morning, afternoon or evening) as recorded in the 1851 religious census

Church of England

At the time the enquiry into education was carried out, provision for elementary education in England and Wales was largely in the hands of religious societies. Although their hours were restricted to six and a half per day, children as young as eight years old were still employed in factories, and for many of them the Sunday School was their chief means of learning basic skills. For the education enquiry, enumerators in the main 1851 Census were instructed to enquire, on their first visit to every house when delivering the household schedule, whether any school was carried on there and, if so, a form was left to be filled in by the heads or keepers of the schools. The information asked for was extensive. It covered the number of schools, their religious and secular affiliations, their income and expenditure and date when they were established; the number and sex of teachers and their pay and level of training; the number, sex and age of pupils on the books and attendance on the census day; the subject taught and the number of pupils receiving it. There was also a range of questions concerned with evening schools for adults. Unfortunately, much of the information collected was never published and much of what did appear was condensed into short summaries or expressed on a sample basis. As the original manuscript returns no longer exist it is not now possible to go back and re-work the material[4].

The censuses from 1861 to 1901

In Scotland civil registration of births, deaths and marriages began in 1855 under the control of a Registrar General for Scotland and a separate Act, in 1860, gave him responsibility for taking a census in 1861. The organisation which he set up followed similar lines to the system in England and Wales. Although there have been minor differences, between both the schedules and the analysis of the results, collaboration between the two Registrars General has generally been sufficiently close for basic tables to be prepared on a Great Britain basis.

In England and Wales there was little change in the content of the census schedules in the decades between 1861 and 1911. These years are chiefly remarkable for the increasing sophistication of the tables in the reports and for the commentaries by the Registrars General and their statistical superintendents. Thus the 1861 general report included a section on the laws regulating the growth of nations and a short note, supported by tables, on the area and population of the British Empire compiled from the census returns of British colonies and possessions. It is significant that the influence of Malthus was such that this report in 1861, more than sixty years after the publication of the first edition of his Essay on Population, also included a trenchant criticism of his theory.

Towards the end of the century concern about overcrowding led, in 1891 and again in 1901, to a question on the number of rooms per house for those households with fewer than five rooms. The 1901 Census also enquired into the number of people in certain industries working in their own homes, and in the report females with an occupation were for the first time tabulated by marital status.

Questions had already been asked about blind and deaf-and-dumb people in the 1851 and 1861 Censuses and, in 1871, lunatics and imbeciles or idiots were added to the list. In 1901, 'idiot' was replaced by 'feeble-minded'. Enquiries into infirmities were not repeated after 1911, it being finally accepted that the census was not a suitable or reliable medium for getting information of this kind. As the Registrar General had commented in his report for 1881:

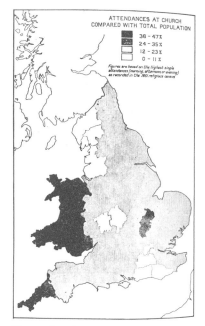

Nonconformists

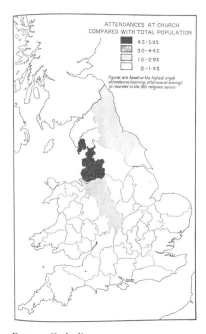

Roman Catholic

It is against human nature to expect a mother to admit her young child to be an idiot, however much she may fear this to be true. Openly to acknowledge the fact is to abandon all hope.

The 1911 Census

The 1911 Census was marked by a major step forward in the processing of information. Punch-card and mechanical sorting by machines transformed the handling of the data collected in the schedules and opened up the possibility of new and more detailed analyses. It speeded up the whole operation because, after preliminary coding, the data were transferred direct to the cards from the individual household schedules. The illustration gives an example of a card used in the 1911 Census. It had 36 columns in which operators recorded the coded information by punching round holes in the appropriate numbered positions so that a machine could then sort all the cards with holes in the selected positions. Further machines were used for counting and tabulating the pre-sorted cards. The new methods of processing not only made it possible for the results of the census to be presented in greater detail, but also had the great advantage of enabling data to be re-sorted to overcome some of the problems associated with the realignment of local government boundaries at the end of the nineteenth century. This made them much more useful for administrative purposes.

A punch card used for processing the 1911 Census data

The most important innovation in the census questions in 1911 was the special enquiry into fertility of marriage. It is interesting to reflect that, during the long period in which both the census and the Registrar General's office had been in existence, the interest in vital statistics was mainly in mortality and morbidity: interest in fertility came much later. Some of the reasons for this are discussed in Chapter 11 on population. The birth rate had in fact been falling since the late 1870s, and the Registrar General had already suggested in his Annual Report for 1904 that some thought might perhaps be given to including more details in the birth registration about the ages of the parents, the date of their marriage and the number of children born.

War broke out in 1914 and, as more and more of the GRO staff were drawn into war service, so it became more difficult to prepare the usual reports. The tabulations of the fertility data in the 1911 Census were very lengthy and the first volume of results was not published until 1917. The second volume, which contained a report as well as the tables, had to wait until 1923.

> In the Records branch of the Office there has been a marked increase in the normal demand for copies of certificates of births and marriages due to the war, and arrangements have had to be made to meet a continuous rush of applications under a system of gratuitous verification of births, deaths, and marriages, the institution of which became necessary early in the day for the benefit of soldiers and their dependants and for War Office purposes in connexion with pensions and "effects." To the Statistical branch in the main two important pieces of additional work have fallen; firstly, the creation of a Central Register of War Refugees under the Order in Council of the 29th November, 1914, and, secondly, the organization and superintendence of the National Register set up by the National Registration Act, 1915, both of which have involved the employment of a large number of temporary clerks, male and female, not included in the figures I shall now mention.

Wartime activities 1914–18: the National Register and the Central Register of War refugees. (*Seventy-seventh Report of the Registrar General, 1914*)

The census in the inter-war years

The 1920 Census Act, unlike its predecessors, was a permanent enactment applicable to all future censuses in Great Britain. It did not cover Northern Ireland where each census still has to be specifically enacted. Two important procedural changes were also made at this time. The first provided for separate confidential returns to be made to the enumerator by people within a household, instead of through the 'head of household', if they so wished. The second placed the local registrars directly under the instructions of headquarters instead of the superintendent registrars. The regulations, however, provided for the appointment in each area of a census advisory officer who was very often the superintendent registrar acting in an honorary capacity.

In the years immediately following the First World War there was growing concern with traffic problems and the tendency of people to live in suburban residential areas. The 1921 Census therefore included a question on place of work to help measure the daily movement of people to and from work. There were also questions for the first time about the ages and numbers of children under 16 and about full or part-time education. Free and compulsory elementary education had been introduced at the end of the nineteenth century and the further development of secondary education followed at the beginning of the twentieth century. From 1921 onwards the census introduced increasingly detailed questions to monitor the educational qualifications of the population.

Occupation and social class

A major development during the inter-war years was the further revision and refinement of the occupational classification and its grouping into social classes. The 1911 Census had already begun asking separate questions on occupation and industry but the occupational classification derived from it was still partly industry-based. The 1921 Census questions amplified and clarified the distinction between 'occupation' and 'industry' and the improved information made possible a new and separate classification of industries: this involved a complete re-casting of what had formerly been known as the occupational classification.

This, in its turn, led to re-allocation of the new occupational groups to social class. The history of the discussions and controversies leading up to the five social classes adopted in the Census of 1921, which have so dominated demographic analysis in the twentieth century, is long and complex. In the early days of the GRO, Farr published Life Tables of 'healthy districts' as a yardstick for comparing expectation of life in different communities. But it was clear that, even within these healthy districts, mortality, particularly of the children of the well-to-do, varied substantially and that there were other factors operating related to occupation, poverty and overcrowding. As already described, Farr in 1851 therefore set about analysing mortality according to occupation which the GRO published, and continues to publish, under the title of the *Decennial Supplement of Occupational Mortality in England and Wales*.

There was also a continuing interest from life insurance societies in the differential mortality of the various strata of society. The directors of the National Life Assurance Society were 'contemplating the formation of a more extended plan of Educational and other Endowments' and asked Charles Ansell to look at the mortality rates prevailing among children in the Upper

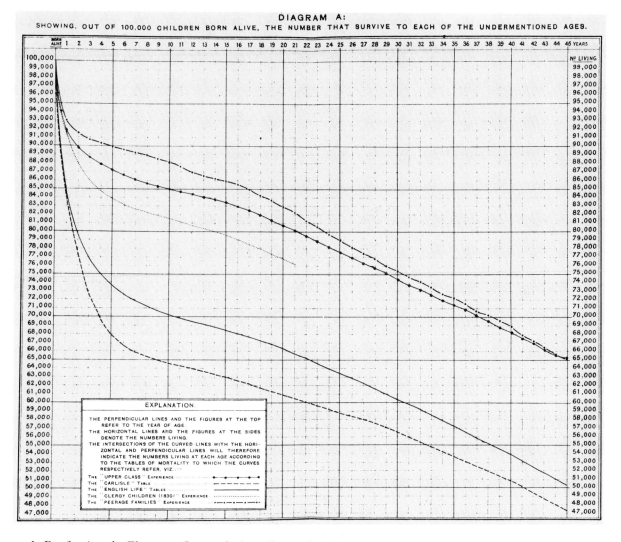

DIAGRAM A:

SHOWING, OUT OF 100,000 CHILDREN BORN ALIVE, THE NUMBER THAT SURVIVE TO EACH OF THE UNDERMENTIONED AGES.

EXPLANATION.

THE PERPENDICULAR LINES AND THE FIGURES AT THE TOP REFER TO THE YEAR OF AGE.
THE HORIZONTAL LINES AND THE FIGURES AT THE SIDES DENOTE THE NUMBERS LIVING.
THE INTERSECTIONS OF THE CURVED LINES WITH THE HORIZONTAL AND PERPENDICULAR LINES WILL THEREFORE INDICATE THE NUMBERS LIVING AT EACH AGE ACCORDING TO THE TABLES OF MORTALITY TO WHICH THE CURVES RESPECTIVELY REFER. VIZ.—

THE "UPPER CLASS" EXPERIENCE
THE "CARLISLE" TABLE
THE "ENGLISH LIFE" TABLES
THE "CLERGY CHILDREN (1830)" EXPERIENCE
THE "PEERAGE FAMILIES" EXPERIENCE

and Professional Classes. One of the charts he prepared is reproduced here; the 'Carlisle' life table which he mentions is referred to later in Chapter 9 on health statistics.

The grouping of the occupations developed by Farr into social classes was a somewhat later development. In an address to the Royal Statistical Society in 1887, Mr. Noel Humphreys, the Assistant Registrar General, stated that it was 'urgently desirable that we should know more of the rates of mortality prevailing in the different strata of society'. But it was more than twenty years later in 1911 before Dr T H C Stevenson, the statistical superintendent at the GRO, introduced such a classification for the first time when he used it for analysing infant mortality in the Registrar General's Annual Report.

A table of mortality for families in the upper and professional classes.
(C. Ansell, *Statistics of families in the upper and professional classes, 1874*)

This classification was also used for the 1911 Census. The published tables introduced a grouping of occupations 'designed to represent as far as possible different social grades' and the rankings, according to Stevenson, were intended to reflect wealth and culture, the latter being equated with a 'combination of knowledge and skill which enables a person to use his purchasing power wisely'. The classification grouped relatively homogeneous occupations according to the degree of skill involved and the social position implied. The population was divided into eight social groups with the first five being ranked in descending order of social position but, as the prime purpose of the grouping in its early years was to analyse mortality and fertility, the remaining three groups – textile workers, miners and agricultural workers – were considered sufficiently important to be identified separately. At the time of the 1921 Census, Stevenson considered other possible indicators of social position, such as the number of domestic servants kept and the size of tenement, but both these measures were strongly correlated with family size and the classification finally adopted was entirely based on occupation: the first five classes were retained and textile workers, miners and agricultural workers reallocated between them[6,7].

Stevenson was still left with the problem that ranking by social class, even one based on a relatively precise concept such as occupation, is in large measure a subjective exercise depending on a personal view of the circumstances of the time[8]. The esteem in which different skills are held shifts over time. Clerks, for example, who were highly regarded in the nineteenth century, were relegated from Social Class I to Social Class II in 1911 and then to Social Class III in 1931. Before the spread of universal education and the introduction of the typewriter their skills were much in demand. A glance at the private letter book of the Registrar General in the early days of the GRO shows how each letter was carefully copied in a beautifully regular and flowing script by someone who took great pride in his craft.

The census and changing social attitudes

The problem of grouping occupations into social classes illustrates the difficulty of comparing one census with another where definitions and classifications change over time. This conflict between comparability and the need to reflect current social attitudes is one which has continually exercised the minds of the statisticians at the GRO during the 150 years of its existence. The concluding paragraphs of this chapter consider in rather more detail the changing concepts of work and occupation as a further example of the way in which the statistics collected have adapted to social change and to the controversies which were current at the time. It is a good example of the many pitfalls which can trap the unwary researcher who wants to study trends in employment over the past decades.

The very first census, in 1801, set out to collect information on occupation and economic activity. Manufacturing industry was spreading rapidly and it was important to know the number of workers employed in different sectors. The problem, as the first census-takers were soon to find out, was that traditionally the family rather than the individual had been regarded as the economic unit. Chapter 5 has already referred to some of the difficulties experienced in trying to tabulate the replies to the individual occupation question in the 1801 Census and how, in the two subsequent censuses, the question was re-phrased to relate to families. The 1831 Census, however, began to move towards the concept of an individual occupation by also collecting information and presenting tables on the occupations of all males aged twenty and over, all male servants under 20, and all female servants of any age. By the time of the 1841 Census, the family occupations were dropped and individual occupations only were recorded. Some family workers, such as farmers' wives, were included but others, such as the wives of professional men or shopkeepers, were not[9].

The change in the method of collecting data in the 1841 Census in itself reflected a change in attitudes. The census form was addressed to the householder and hence singled out an individual rather than the family, which had been the more traditional approach, and the concept of the individual house-holder became increasingly important in later censuses when questions were asked about kin relationships linked to the head of the household.

The decision to exclude unpaid family workers from the working population in the 1841 Census raised the problem of how to classify them, particularly the very large numbers of women who could hardly be regarded as unoccupied. The census commentaries reflect an ambivalent attitude over whether they should be classified as economically inactive. In the event, the decision to exclude unpaid family workers was reversed in the 1851 Census, and women engaged in domestic duties were recorded in a separate class of occupations rather than among the inactive: the published statistics on the number of occupied women in the active group thus jumps by a million from 1.8 to 2.8 million between 1841 and 1851.

The importance of a wife, mother, mistress of an English family in 1851 (*Census Report, 1851: Vol I Population Tables II*)

The FIFTH CLASS comprises large numbers of the population that have hitherto been held to have no occupation; but it requires no argument to prove that the *wife*, the *mother*, the *mistress* of an *English Family*—fills offices and discharges duties of no ordinary importance; or that children are or should be occupied in filial or household duties, and in the task of education, either at home or at school.

The most important production of a country is its population. And under the institution of marriage, and the actual organization of families, this country has a population of much higher character than countries where polygamy prevails, where the wife is confined at home, and where the management of the household in all its details,—and the care of providing all necessaries,—belong to the husband. ....

.... The child receives nurture, warmth, affection, admonition, education, from a good mother; who, with the child in her arms, is in the eyes of all European nations surrounded by a sanctity which is only adequately expressed in the highest works of art. The fatal effects of living in concubinage—or of a wife sending her child to the Foundling Hospital—neglecting her duties—leaving her children to the care of strangers—are well known; for under such circumstances monogamic nations inevitably fall in arrear, like the races who practise polygamy.

Formerly in this country spinning was carried on extensively as a domestic occupation; ....

Spinning as well as weaving is, however, now generally abandoned, but the household works and processes are still sufficiently numerous; as they include, among large classes of the population, the making and mending of apparel, washing, cooking, cleansing, nursing, teaching, and other offices.

The importance of the duties of a wife is seen in the Anglo-Saxon labourer's cottage—in the clean house, the dry floor, the healthy children and their neat clothes—the husband's comfortable meal, and the enjoyment which, under all difficulties, she manages to shed around her; and is still more strikingly displayed in higher circles. The duties of a wife, a mother, and a mistress of a family can only be efficiently performed by unremitting attention; accordingly it is found that in districts where the women are much employed from home, the children and parents perish in great numbers.

The HUSBAND as well as the HOUSEWIFE in the British Family performs household duties, although he is in all cases classed under other special occupations.

The excerpt from the 1851 Census report (see above) records how the Registrar General justified his decision. The extract is itself a sharp reminder of social change, both in its style of writing and the degree to which Registrars General in the nineteenth century felt they were able to comment on the affairs of the government of the day.

The 1861 Census report emphasises even more firmly that the occupation of wife and mother is the most important in the country. The 1871 Census report again affirms a wife's economic functions in the household but, as the excerpt from the report suggests, the emphasis was beginning to shift. Those who prepared the census schedules were aware that people can be both 'housewives' and carry on other occupations at the same time, and they were confused about how to deal with the problem of

As girls and women of all ages now constitute more than half of the population of England, their occupations are of vital importance. 3,948,527 are wives, and a large proportion of them are mothers. This is a noble and essential occupation, as on it as much as on the husband's labour and watchfulness depend the existence and character of the English race. But in all stages of human progress, women have had, besides these, other employments; among savages they perform the most laborious work; and in Europe now they are seen burdened and toiling in the fields, as women were once found toiling underground in English mines. Engaged in spinning and weaving in the heroic times, in cookery and surgery in the age of chivalry, their employments are now becoming infinitely diversified; a married woman of industry and talent aids her husband in his special occupation, or she follows different lines of her own; even when she has children this is possible, for it is only in a few cases that the whole of a wife's lifetime is filled up with childbearing, nursing, and housekeeping. Women unmarried, always exist in great numbers and will continue to exist at all ages, who devote themselves to works of utility or charity, and to the arts, for which they have a taste, in which they often display extraordinary talent, and for which they get as well remunerated as men. In literature and song women have always excelled. There are certain walks of athletic life from which women are inflexibly excluded; whether with advantage, without drawbacks, it is difficult to say, as many of the finest children are produced by hard-working women. They are also excluded wholly or in great part from the church, the law, and medicine; whether they should be rigidly excluded from these professions, or be allowed—on the principle of freedom of trade—to compete with men, is one of the questions of the day.

Early problems with the classification of occupations; in the 1871 census women have many occupations (*Census Report, 1871: Vol IV General Report and Appendix*)

double-counting. The 1881 Census once again excluded household work from the definition of economic activity. In 1911, the schedule was again modified to include all family workers, male and female, among the economically active, and only those engaged in housework alone were excluded.

The unpaid labour of family workers was not the only problem which arose in the census. Whereas today we are familiar with the concepts of childhood, retirement, unemployment and student status, the early censuses were not. At first everybody was included in the occupational classification. The retired were allocated to their previous occupations and students to their potential ones: even lunatics and prisoners were ascribed to an occupation, and unemployment was taken to be only a temporary break from an occupied and active status. Changes came slowly and it was not until 1881 that most retired people were classed as unoccupied. Childhood was finally given a status of its own in 1891, when the cut-off point for classification into occupations was given as 10 years and over, this being the age at which children could be employed in factories. In 1901 students were classed as unoccupied. Some attempt had been made at the end of the nineteenth century to segregate the unemployed but it took the post-war depression years, at the time of the 1931 Census, before they were separately classified.

The above examples illustrate some of the problems underlying the census classifications which make comparisons between censuses so difficult. With hindsight it is easy to criticise the statisticians of the time and to forget that, during the nineteenth century, they were living in a different society. In trying to define personal occupation, for example, they were up against the problem that the concept implied various attributes – separation of home and workplace, individual mobility, cash earnings, and continuous employment – and none of these were firmly established at either end of the social scale at the beginning of the nineteenth century[10]. One result of their endeavours was that, by the end of the century, they had succeeded in identifying only those occupations in which activities were gainful as distinct from those that were productive. Some of the consequences of the statistics which they produced and the definitions they used have been long lasting. The concept of the national income, for example, is based mainly on cash transactions and with scant attention to the importance of unpaid economic activity: nineteenth century census definitions thus helped to shape twentieth century thinking and the policies which flowed from it. Definitions and classifications inevitably reflect the preconceptions of those who devise them and, once devised, they in turn produce inescapable conclusions and policies.

References

1. Michael McDowall. William Farr and the Study of Occupational Mortality, in *Population Trends*, No. 31. 1983, London, HMSO.

2. David M Thompson. The Religious Census of 1851, in *The Census and Social Structure*, ed. Richard Lawton. 1978, London, Cass.

3. J M Goldstrom. The Education Census of 1851, in *The Census and Social Structure*, ed. Richard Lawton. 1978, London, Cass.

4. T H C Stevenson. The Vital Statistics of Wealth and Poverty, in the *Journal of the Royal Statistical Society*, Vol. XCI. 1929, London.

5. Richard Leete and John Fox. Registrar General's social classes: origins and uses, in *Population Trends*, No. 8. 1977, London, HMSO.

6. G F P Boston. *Occupation, Industry, Social Class and Socio-Economic Group, 1911–1981*. 1984, London, OPCS.

7. S R S Szreter. The genesis of the Registrar General's social classification of occupations, in the *British Journal of Sociology*, Vol. XXXV, No. 4.

8. Catherine Hakim. Census Reports as Documentary Evidence, in *The Sociological Review*, Vol. 28, No. 3. 1980, University of Keele.

9. C Davies. Making Sense of the Census in Britain and the USA, in *The Sociological Review*, Vol. 28, No. 3. 1980, University of Keele.

The census: the last fifty years

7

National Registration, 1939

The Second World War broke out on 3 September 1939 and less than a month later, on 29 September, the population of the United Kingdom was enumerated, under the direction of the Registrars General, so that national registers might be compiled as a war-time general security measure. Preparations for this 'National Register', had already begun at the end of 1938 and were virtually complete by April 1939. Had the country been at peace, these preparations would have been used for a 1941 Census of Population but the disruption caused by the war made this impracticable. Some of the statistics from the enumeration were published in 1944 but they are not comparable with those in the censuses. The enumeration itself was used for issuing national Identity Cards and as a basis for supporting a variety of other wartime measures such as food and clothes rationing and the deployment of labour in military and other essential industries and services.

National Registration was abolished in February 1952 but, in the meantime, the identity numbers and the registers had been

A National Register was compiled under the direction of the Registrar General in 1939 as a wartime security measure, and was used for issuing identity cards to the population

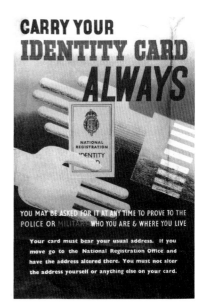

NATIONAL REGISTRATION

| NIGK | 18 | 6 |

SMITH
James H

1. This Identity Card must be carefully preserved. You may need it under conditions of national emergency for important purposes. You must not lose it or allow it to be stolen. If, nevertheless, it is stolen or completely lost, you must report the fact in person at any local National Registration Office.
2. You may have to show your Identity Card to persons who are authorised by law to ask you to produce it.
3. You must not allow your Identity Card to pass into the hands of unauthorised persons or strangers. Every grown up person should be responsible for the keeping of his or her Identity Card. The Identity Card of a child should be kept by the parent or guardian or person in charge of the child for the time being.
4. Anyone finding this Card must hand it in at a Police Station or National Registration Office.

(47062) 100M 4/39

NATIONAL REGISTRATION

| NIGK | 18 | 6 |

SMITH
James H

DO NOTHING WITH THIS PART
UNTIL YOU ARE TOLD

Full Postal Address of Above Person :—

_____

_____

_____

(Signed) _____

Date _____

CARRY YOUR
IDENTITY CARD
ALWAYS

NATIONAL
REGISTRATION
IDENTITY

YOU MAY BE ASKED FOR IT AT ANY TIME TO PROVE TO THE POLICE OR MILITARY WHO YOU ARE & WHERE YOU LIVE

Your card must bear your usual address. If you move go to the National Registration Office and have the address altered there. You must not alter the address yourself or anything else on your card.

used to prepare the National Health Service Central Register (NHSCR). For those people who held national Identity Cards the number on the card became, and still remains, their NHS number. Newly-born children are issued with NHS numbers at the time of birth registration and immigrants and anyone whose original number cannot be traced are allocated numbers on a different system as the need arises. The NHSCR is a register of NHS patients kept up-to-date from returns sent by the local registrars of births and deaths and family practitioner committees (FPCs). Transfers of patients between FPCs are recorded and from this information it is possible to monitor internal migration in England and Wales for use in making the population estimates.

The NHSCR is used for a variety of research purposes, particularly medical, and some of these are described in later chapters. The register of patients in England and Wales is housed in Southport and it is interesting to note that the staff, amounting to about 600 people, now occupy a building which used to be a

An extract from the 1881 Census enumerator's return for Birkdale Hydro, the building now occupied by the NHSCR. It reflects the ages and occupational background of the visitors who used to stay there.

				The undermentioned Houses are situate within the Boundaries of the			
~ough of	Municipal Ward of	Parliamentary Borough of			Town or Village or Hamlet of	Urban Sanitary District of	
						Birkdale S.D.	

	NAME and Surname of each Person	RELATION to Head of Family	CON-DITION as to Marriage	AGE last Birthday of Males	AGE last Birthday of Females	Rank, Profession, or OCCUPATION	
	Samuel L. Halliwell	Boarder (Patient)	M	50		Cotton Spinner	
	Elizabeth Andrew	do	Un		51	Legacy under Fathers will	
	Joshua Hoyle	do	W?	70		Cotton Spinner	
	Robert do	do do	M	44		do do	
	Ann Jane do	do do	Un		18	Daur of Robert Hoyle	
	Alice do	do	do		38	Joshua	
	Robert Bushell (Rev)	do do	M	53		Methodist Missionary Sec?	
	Emma A. Bushell	do do	do		56	wife	
	John Evans	do do	Un	47		Income in Stocks	
	George Marsden	do do	do	64		do	
	James Boothroyd	do do	M	57		Draper	
	Isaac Holmes	do	do	69		Cotton Merchant	
	Sarah do	do do	do		56	" wife	
	William H. Soulby	do do	Un	30		" "	
	Mary A. Newton	do do	M		61	wife of a Cotton Spinner	
	Fannie Hall	do do	do		39	Wine Merchants wife	
	Bertha G. Cooke	do do	Un		24	Russian Genyal Mer. Daur	
	David Woodhouse	serv	M	38		Batman (Domestic Serv)	
	Hannah do	"	"			Bathwoman do	
	Alice Boud	"	Un			do do	
	Ell.. Sele	"	"			Mrs Clarkhous Housemaid do	
	Hannah Moore	Boarder	M		61	Physicians wife	
	Mary A. Tomlinson	do (Patient)	Un		64	Annuitant	
	C. Elliade	do do	do	26		Gen? Turkish Mr?	
	Samuel P. Clarke	do do	M	34		Provision Merchant	
		Total of Males and Females...			12	13		

'Hydro' where people came to seek the benefits of the sea air in the days when the town had the reputation of being a health resort or spa. The illustration, taken from the 1881 Census enumerator's return for the district (which under the 100 years confidentiality rule has only recently been made available) reflects the ages and occupational background of the visitors who used to stay there.

The census: 1951 to 1981

Five censuses have been held since the end of the Second World War. Although the Census Act of 1920 did not lay down when a census should be taken it specified that it should not be less than five years after the preceding one. Accordingly, in 1966, a sample census was taken only five years after the one in 1961. Plans were also made for a census in 1976 but the squeeze on public expenditure led to its being abandoned.

The 1951 Census was wider in scope than earlier ones, particularly the 1931 Census which was taken at a time of severe economic depression and collected only basic information. In the intervening twenty years there had been many social and legislative changes and the number of questions asked in the schedules grew steadily from 1951 until 1971.

The plans for the 1971 Census were ambitious. The field force had, up to this time, been built around the registration

Women working on the National Register in 1939. One of their tasks was to check up the men who failed to register for military service

service, with superintendent registrars and registrars being specifically mentioned in the Census Act, 1920. It became clear, however, that with the growth in population and number of households, any increase in questions and other extra tasks would overburden the registration service. Moreover, since the late 1950s, there had been a steady flow of immigrants into the country, many of whom might find difficulty or be apprehensive about filling in census forms. A new census supervisory structure was therefore created and special attention given to the field organisation, which was increased by 50 per cent compared with the 1961 Census. Census supervisors were engaged and trained to recruit census officers (many of whom still came from the registration service) and to take control of the census field operations, each supervisor being responsible for an area containing about half a million people. For the first time Ordnance Survey maps were issued to enumerators; in previous censuses a description or tracing of the boundary and a description of the enumeration district had had to

The 21 questions in the 1981 Census

The 21 Questions in the 1981 Census

Population items
1   Name
2   Sex
3   Date of birth
4   Marital status (single, married, remarried, divorced, widowed)
5* Relationship in household (husband/wife/, son/daughter, other: specified)
6   Whereabouts on census night
7   Usual address (including postcode)
8   Usual address: 1 year ago (including postcode)
9   Country of birth (present name of country)
10 Whether working, retired, housewife, etc., last week (full, part, etc.)
11* Name and business of employer
12* Occupation (includes description of work)
13 Employment status (apprentice, supervisory role, self-employed)
14* Address of place of work (including postcode)
15* Daily journey to work (train, tube, bus, van, foot, etc.)
16* Degrees, professional and vocational qualifications

Housing Items
H1 Number of rooms
H2 Tenure (freehold, leasehold, renting, other)
H3 Amenities (fixed bath or shower connected, WC)
H4 Shared household
H5 Cars and vans (number)

There was an additional question in Wales asking whether people speak Welsh; and, if so, whether they speak English and read or write Welsh.
    * Questions marked with an asterisk were included on all the forms, but only a 10 per cent sample of the replies were processed.

suffice. The purpose of the maps was to enable enumerators to reference properties precisely on what is known as the national grid, or series of squares now shown on all Ordnance Survey maps, but the maps proved so useful that they were issued again in the 1981 Census[1].

A list of the questions asked in the 1981 Census is shown in the illustration. Their number was much reduced compared with 1971, partly because of the unpopularity of long and complex forms and the high cost of processing them but also because other sources, such as the General Household Survey and the Labour Force Survey, had become available[2]. A question on ethnic origin was proposed and extensively tested on a voluntary basis in the London Borough of Haringay in 1979, but many people refused to answer it and it became clear that a compulsory question might not give usable answers. There were further discussions with the Commission for Racial Equality and other interested organisations, followed by a full-scale debate in Parliament which resulted in a decisive vote against including the question and the proposal was dropped[3].

Computerisation was introduced for the first time in 1961 using the Royal Army Pay Corp computer at Winchester but it was not until the sample census of 1966 that the Office had its own computer. In 1981 the data from the schedules (excluding names and addresses) was keyed directly on to magnetic tape.

The 1971 Census was held at a time when there was considerable national anxiety about the possible misuse of

A store of computer tapes holding census data

information held on computers, and various organisations such as the National Council of Civil Liberties, as well as a number of MPs who were members of the Liberal Party, organised a campaign against the compulsory nature of the census. Under the Census Act is is illegal for the Census Office to disclose information about individuals but, despite absolute guarantees given by Michael Reed, the Registrar General, there still remained the lurking fear that Government departments might perhaps pass information from one to another. The publicity given to the issue helped to bring it into the open and, more recently, the 1984 Data Protection Act has ensured that all census information on living individuals held on computer is not disclosed to anybody else.

The use of sampling

One of the main features of the post-war censuses was the use of sampling either at the enumeration or the processing stage. The report on the 1951 Census saw the early publication, in 1952, of a one per cent sample of the more important results much in advance of most of the final figures. The 1961 Census introduced sampling at the time of enumeration by distributing a short form, with basic questions only, to all householders and a longer form to a ten per cent sample asking for more details on economic activity, education, household composition and migration. Checks on the sample showed substantial biases, particularly among the elderly and aliens, possibly because enumerators hesitated to issue long forms to those who might find it difficult to fill them in. The 1966 Census brought a further experiment in sampling by approaching only those households living in one out of ten dwellings. This too produced problems because of a shortfall in the sample of dwellings. The 1971 Census again used sampling but only at the processing stage. As in 1951, an early summary of the main results was published based on a one per cent sample of returns. In addition a one in ten sample of the data needed for some of the more complex analyses was drawn from the computer records, so avoiding the pitfalls of sampling in the field. Moreover it meant that the full information for answering questions of any sub-group or sample of the population was available should it be needed. A similar ten per cent sample was taken in 1981 but, in the interests of speedy results for the census as a whole, there was no one per cent initial sample[4].

A new and most important development in the 1971 and 1981 Censuses was their use as sampling frames for a longitudinal study. This type of study looks at the flow or sequence of events occurring over a span of time to particular groups or 'cohorts' of

Above, the Letter patent of the appointment of the first Registrar General. Below, the great seal of William IV, attached to the Letter patent.

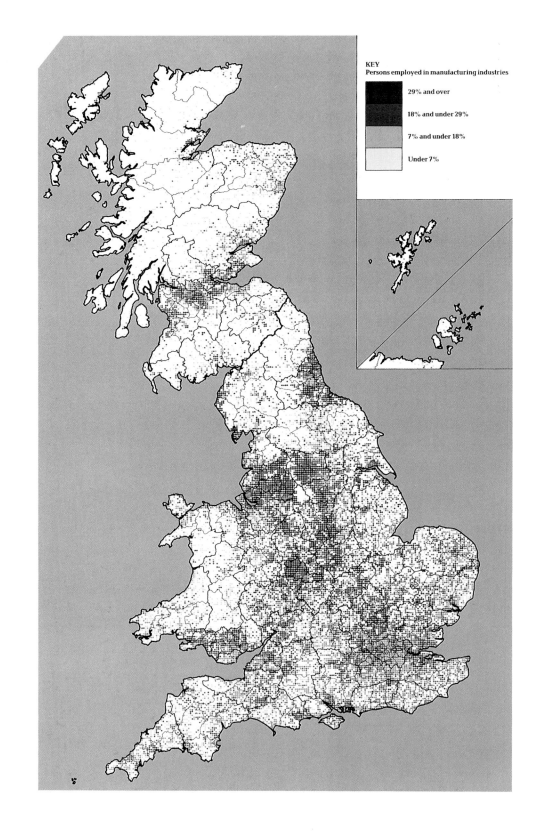

KEY
Persons employed in manufacturing industries

29% and over

18% and under 29%

7% and under 18%

Under 7%

Changing styles of mapping techniques. This page, a mid-nineteenth century map of Great Britain, showing the distribution of occupations in the 1851 Census. Opposite, a late twentieth century map of Great Britain, showing the distribution of persons employed in manufacturing industries in the 1981 Census.

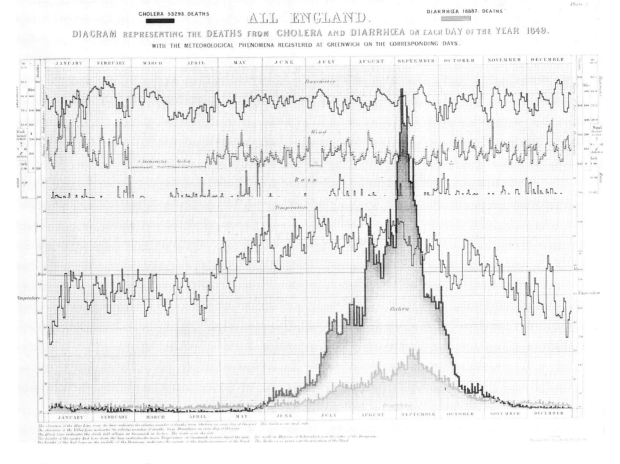

A mid-nineteenth century diagram, representing deaths from cholera and diarrhoea on each day of the year 1849. (*Registrar General's report on cholera in England, 1849*)

individuals. The census is a mine of information on the social and economic characteristics of the population of the country but, until 1981, information about individuals in each census was kept separate and not linked to any information in a previous census. Analysis therefore had to be confined to cross-sectional data, or events occurring at one particular point of time. Longitudinal analysis on the other hand can study the past circumstances which have led up to an event. Research on mortality, for example, can be greatly helped if the circumstances of a death can be given perspective by linking it to earlier events in a person's life and to the home and working conditions which provide the lifetime background. Similarly, the birth of a child is not an isolated event in the life-cycle of a couple, but is related to their social and economic characteristics before the birth. William Farr, as far back as 1839, had already perceived the importance of cohort analysis and, in commenting on tables of mortality for different sections of the population, went so far as to say that the government had a duty to establish longitudinal studies[5]:

> To determine a question of this sort it would be necessary to take a large number of individuals, as 400,000 or 500,000, indiscriminately selected from all ranks and orders of the community, and to trace their lives from the moment of their birth, marking the exact period of the demise of each individual . . . But governments, which alone have the means of framing tables on an adequate scale, and with the necessary precautions, have been singularly inattentive to their duty in this respect.

It was over a century later before the type of study envisaged by Farr was set up. Four birth dates in a year were selected and the records of individuals born on these days were marked in the 1971 Census and in the NHSCR; they were then followed up in the 1981 Census. As described in a later chapter on health statistics (Chapter 10), a number of medical research studies are based on the linked data; the study is also now used for a wide range of demographic and other research studies.

OPCS brings together the data in a form which ensures their complete confidentiality. No information about identified individuals can leave OPCS but there is provision for statistical tables to be produced within OPCS by researchers, such as in the major collaborative programme with the Social Statistics Research Unit at City University[6].

Are there alternatives to the census?

The 1981 Census in England and Wales cost (at 1980 prices) £45 million, or rather less than £1 per head of population. In addition to the large numbers of permanent staff employed by OPCS in planning, processing and analysing the census, over 100,000 enumerators were employed on a temporary basis for about 60–70 hours spread over a period of two months. The total output of tables, in both 1971 and 1981, ran to some one and a half million pages published during the course of the succeeding three years[7].

The carrying out of a census is thus a very large and costly operation. At present it takes place only once every ten years and, by the end of that time the results can be very out-of-date. Moreover, as circumstances change, they do not necessarily provide precisely what is needed by their users and, although the OPCS may be able to provide special tabulations, these cost extra money and time. In future, if the necessary legislation were to be passed, it might be possible, as in the United States, to give users quicker and more flexible access to the census by means of computer tapes based on samples with names removed and certain precautions taken to ensure that individuals are not likely to be identifiable. Plans are already being prepared for another census in 1991 but the heavy call on resources raises the question of whether there are viable alternatives. The paragraphs which follow examine the purpose of the census today and consider some of the ways in which other countries meet similar needs.

Traditionally its main purpose has been to count heads, a kind of national stock-taking of our most important national resource. The history of the census in England and Wales since it began in 1801 has shown, however, that governments have been increasingly concerned with basic information about the characteristics of this population, such as age, sex, marital status, place of birth, economic activity, health and housing. More recent topics have included change of address, car ownership, place of work and educational qualifications.

This information is used for a variety of different purposes by both central and local government. For example, central government pays out a great deal of money by way of rate support grants to local authorities and grants to health authorities. One of the main criteria for sharing out this money is the kind of population in each local area and it is therefore critically important to obtain accurate statistics for small areas. In between censuses population estimates are made for local areas in England and Wales by OPCS by using births and deaths registrations for each area combined with such data as exist on movements between areas. Mention has already been made of the way migration can be measured by using the NHSCR information on transfers between FPCs, and estimates are also prepared from the electoral registers and local authority housing lists. The results, when set alongside subsequent census results, have often been very inexact.

Local authorities themselves use census data for many planning purposes, particularly housing, transport and education. Social service departments need small area statistics to identify special groups, such as old people living alone and one-parent families. Today this information is so important that small area statistics derived from the census, which were first published only in 1961, are now prepared by OPCS for local wards and each of the 100,000 or so enumeration districts. The tables are available in machine-readable form, in microfiche or as printed copy.

The census results are used as a basis for very many other national and regional statistics and, subject to strict rules on confidentiality of details about individuals, for a multitude of research analyses. For many types of analysis, the census is at present the only source for getting accurate information about specific and very often quite small groups of people and relating together all the various details about them. For instance, not only is it a principal source for estimating the number of one-parent families, but also how many children they have, the kind of homes they live in, whether any of the family members are employed and what educational qualifications they have.

Experience has shown that the census, compulsorily addressed to the whole population, can be most successful when the questions are few, simple and non-controversial, and that information which is not needed in the fine detail only possible from a very large survey can often be more satisfactorily obtained from smaller sample surveys, particularly where interviews or longer postal questionnaires are more appropriate. With the merger of the Social Survey and the GRO in 1970, OPCS acquired the means of doing this (see Chapter 8).

Many countries already conduct regular general purpose surveys which can be used for cross-analysis of different household characteristics. Canada's Labour Force Survey approaches 30,000 households and the United States Current Population Survey 50,000 households each month. Both countries also carry out censuses every ten years. In Germany a 'micro-census' is conducted on a one per cent sample of households every April, supplemented by a further 0.1 per cent in each of the three subsequent quarters. Although the sample is complemented by a population register, it has not been found a satisfactory replacement for the traditional census.

Britain, in 1970, also started a continuous multi-purpose survey, the General Household Survey, which currently approaches 12,500 households a year on a voluntary basis. More recently, in 1973, the Labour Force Survey has been established as part of a series carried out for the European Community and now covers 0.5 per cent of all households. Both surveys are described in more detail in the next chapter. There are in addition numbers of other surveys, records, lists and registers carried out and maintained by various government departments, but the data are collected mainly for administering particular organisations and programmes. They may, for example, be able to tell something about those who attend schools or pay taxes or work in factories but, unlike the census and the multi-purpose surveys, they contain nothing about their wider family circumstances.

Some countries, notably the Scandinavians, maintain what are sometimes called population registers. Denmark consequently no longer sees the need to conduct full-scale censuses. Population registers, based on unique individual identification numbers, contain regularly updated lists of people resident in the country with addresses and some classificational detail (for example, sex, date of birth and marital status). This data base not only makes possible up-to-date population counts but it can be used for studying the inter-relationships between, and changes in, the many social and economic factors affecting society.

These registers however involve both technical and political problems. The technical problems concern the methods of establishing accurate linkage and of ensuring that records are kept up-to-date. Norway and Sweden, for example, now use a full-scale census mainly as a check on their registers. The political factors involve the need to introduce safeguards to protect personal details. The issue of confidentiality, particularly when information is collected compulsorily, is one of special concern and will play a major part in any discussion on the future of the census. The political objections have been particularly strong in Britain and, since the scrapping of the wartime National Register in 1952, there has been no comprehensive population register, although there are a number of special purpose registers such as those for National Insurance, National Health Service and driving licences. There is also the Electoral Register, and in 1976–79, a special committee considered possible ways of enhancing it to improve annual population estimates at the local level. The idea proposed was that, in addition to the list of people eligible to vote, the householder should also be required to include the names of other people in the household, possibly with additional information such as sex and date of birth. The idea fell to the ground because local authorities were not prepared to see the scheme operated under central control and, if they themselves ran it, there could be no guarantee that the results would be of uniform quality[8]. Instead the local authorities pressed for a mid-term census in 1986 but, as happened with the earlier proposal for a 1976 Census, the Government decided that the cost and burden on the public could not be justified. The next census, for which careful preparations are now being made, is therefore planned for 1991, but this date is still years ahead and in the meantime other political factors, such as the possibility of a poll tax for local revenue, may radically alter the kind of information which the Government may need at the local level.

References

1. Census 1971, England and Wales. *General Report, Part 2: Administration, Fieldwork, Processing.* 1983, OPCS, London.

2. Philip Redfern. Census 1981 – an historical and international perspective, in *Population Trends* No. 23. 1981, London, HMSO.

3. Ken Sillitoe. Ethnic Origin: the Search for a Question, in *Population Trends* No. 13. 1978, London, HMSO.

4. Philip Redfern. Op. cit.

5. W Farr. Vital Statistics, in *A statistical account of the British Empire*, Vol 1, ed McCulloch. 1839, J R Charles Knight and Co.

6. Audrey Brown and John Fox. OPCS Longitudinal Study: ten years on, in *Population Trends* No. 37. 1984, London, HMSO.

7. A R Thatcher. The 1981 Census of Population in England and Wales, in the *Journal of the Royal Statistical Society*, series A, Vol. 147, pt. 2. 1984, London, RSS.

8. A R Thatcher. Discussion on a paper presented by R. Black on a Voluntary Population Survey, in *Proceedings of the Royal Statistical Society*, Vol. 148, Pt. IV. 1985, London, RSS.

Social Surveys

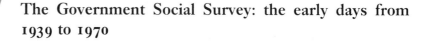

The Government Social Survey: the early days from 1939 to 1970

The Social Survey Division of the OPCS had its origins in the Wartime Social Survey, which came into being as a wartime expedient, but then survived into the post-war period because it had shown that it was too useful to do without[1]. Social Survey Division now carries out the main continuous surveys needed by government as well as a wide variety of one-off or ad hoc surveys and it also acts as a centre of advice on survey methods and management. The description which follows looks at some of the major developments during its existence over what is now nearly a half century.

During the early days of the Second World War, the Government set up a Ministry of Information (MOI), part of whose function was to monitor the state of 'public morale', and the Wartime Social Survey was created to supplement existing sources of information, such as the Gallup Poll and other surveys carried out by Mass Observation and the British Institute of Public Opinion. At first, although funded by the MOI, it was an independent organisation under Professor Arnold Plant operating from the London School of Economics. It quickly came under attack by journalists such as Ritchie Calder who accused its survey teams of 'prying around and asking a lot of silly questions about morale and upsetting the public'. Many people objected to what was regarded as an invasion of privacy and the interviewers themselves became known as 'Cooper's Snoopers' after Arnold Duff Cooper, the Minister of Information. Criticism of the organisation finally led to its becoming part of the MOI with its role being confined to work explicitly commissioned by government departments.

After the reorganisation the surveys reflected the immediate administrative needs of wartime government. Some of the titles make strange reading today. There was, for example, an early survey for the Board of Trade into corset stocks and needs, 'with special reference to the allocation of steel for these garments'. A later study, in 1943, investigated current needs and shortages in domestic brushes and brooms. There were a number of surveys of food consumption – the diets of young people aged 14–18, the methods used for cooking vegetables, the success of the publicity campaign to eat more potatoes, typical wartime meals of housewives, industrial workers and schoolchildren and so on. One early survey was designed to find out why women were not responding to the recruitment campaign for the ATS (the Auxiliary Territorial Service) and another investigated public reaction to the campaign to prevent the spread of venereal disease. A series of short studies dealt with the domestic problems of working women, housewives' auxiliary occupations, jobs done at home by working men, shopping and transport difficulties, health and the use of canteens. From the beginning of 1944 the Survey of Sickness studied the prevalence of illness in the general population. This important innovative study is referred to later in Chapter 10 on health statistics.

The usefulness of social surveys and the expertise which had been developed in sampling techniques and interviewing methods led the post-war government to keep the organisation in being under the title of the Government Social Survey. Accustomed as we now are to the sophistication of present-day surveys, it is difficult to realise just how limited were the methods and expertise of social surveys in these early days. Although the staff were relatively inexperienced and unqualified, they themselves were aware of the shortcomings of the methods they had to use to produce, often in a very short time, the information requested.

In the post-war period, when the new Labour Government was actively pursuing its policy of setting up the welfare state, information was needed on a wide range of topics. The list of surveys includes titles such as road safety, recruitment to mining, pneumoniosis, cot bedding, shopping hours, blood transfusion, crockery stocks and domestic fuel, to name just a few. One survey concerned the likely take-up of Campaign Stars and Medals. Originally it was thought that it might be necessary to strike as many medals as there were people entitled to them. As this covered anyone in the Forces who had served in an overseas campaign as well as certain civilians who had been employed in the Defence Services, the total number was estimated at over nineteen million. In 1947, however, the Social Survey was asked to try to find how many people would be likely to apply and, in January 1948, it reported that the proportion would be only between 30 and 40 per cent. In the middle of the following year it carried out an evaluation of the survey and its methods and came to the gratifying conclusion that the prediction was correct. There had thus been a very considerable saving to the exchequer.

In 1951 the first post-war Conservative Government reduced

The needs of wartime government are reflected in the posters below. The effectiveness of campaigns was surveyed by the Wartime Social Survey

A notice announcing the availability of campaign stars and medals for men and women in recognition of service in the Second World War. The Wartime Social Survey undertook a survey to estimate the likely demand for these stars and medals.

Campaign Stars and Medals

As already announced in the House of Commons, Campaign Stars and Medals for men and women in recognition of service in the war of 1939-1945 are now available. You are asked to make application for your awards, as soon as possible, on an official card because there have been so many changes of address since the end of the war. The official cards are printed in different colours to distinguish the various Services. *They will be obtainable from all Post Offices until June 30th.*

PLEASE COMPLETE YOUR CARD AND POST IT WITHOUT DELAY.

ARMY

Application cards **printed in black** are for use by ex-members of all branches of the Service, including Women's Services, Home Guard and past and present members of the Supplementary Reserve and T.A.; legal beneficiaries of deceased members; and Officers, Warrant Officers, and next-of-kin of deceased Officers of the Indian Army or R.I.N. (in these last cases, add the letters "I.A." after the name of the unit, but address other correspondence to the Commonwealth Relations Office). Serving personnel of the Regular Army need *not* send in a card, as their awards will be issued through Units.

ROYAL AIR FORCE

Application cards **printed in light blue** are for use by serving personnel, ex-members of all branches, including Women's Services, and legal beneficiaries of deceased members of the Service.

MERCHANT NAVY

Application cards **printed in green** are for use by serving personnel and ex-members of the Service. Application on behalf of deceased members of the Service should be made on a special form obtainable from any Mercantile Marine Office, or by post from the Registrar General of Shipping and Seamen, Llantrisant Road, Llandaff, Cardiff.

CIVILIAN AWARDS

Civilians who have already been notified on Form D.M.7 that they are entitled to the Defence Medal should now complete part B of the form and post it to the Home Office. Civilians who qualified for stars and medals by overseas service with the Army should apply by letter to the Headquarters of their respective organizations. If service was with the R.A.F., applications should be made on a R.A.F. card.

Applicants should notify immediately any change of address which occurs before their awards are received.

ROYAL NAVY Special arrangements, to be announced later, are being made for the issue of Royal Navy awards, as these concern prize money as well as stars and medals.

ISSUED BY H.M. GOVERNMENT

the Social Survey to half its size and the Survey of Sickness had to be dropped in 1952. It was, however, given responsibility for various other important surveys, such as the National Food Survey (NFS) and a number of savings surveys. In particular it became involved in plans for carrying out more consumer expenditure surveys. The most important of these was the continuous Family Expenditure Survey (FES). This was a major statistical development of the 1950s and was particularly significant for the Social Survey because it involved substantial continuous fieldwork and processing capabilities. The survey was originally intended to provide weights for the Retail Price Index (RPI) and the Household Expenditure Survey in 1953–54 was carried out with this purpose in mind. The Cost of Living Advisory Committee had recommended that in future the weights for the RPI should be kept under continuous review and revised annually to reflect changes in living standards. Accordingly the continuous Family Expenditure Survey was begun in 1957.

The FES is a voluntary survey of some 11,000 households in the United Kingdom. Members of selected households keep detailed records of expenditure for 14 consecutive days and also provide information on income. It is widely used for a variety of purposes both by government and by academic researchers who can obtain tapes though the Economic and Social Research Council data archive at the University of Essex after special precautions have been taken to preserve the anonymity of individual households. Because information is gathered on both household income and expenditure, it is an invaluable source for assessing the impact of government fiscal measures on the distribution and redistribution of income and for studying poverty amongst low income groups.

Anyone who frequently goes abroad may well have been asked questions at a seaport or airport by interviewers who approach some 180,000 people each year on behalf of the International Passenger Survey (IPS). Travellers are usually in a hurry and may wonder just why they have been bothered in this way. The IPS, which was started in 1961, is in fact an important source of data for various bodies. It is used to find out the number and characteristics of visitors to Britain and of British visitors overseas, including their estimated expenditure, and thus provides information for the tourist and transport industries and for calculating the tourist component of the balance of payments. It also contributes to the population estimates by measuring the number of those arriving to settle permanently in this country and those leaving to settle permanently abroad.

The FES and the IPS, together with the prolific output of ad hoc surveys in the two decades following the end of the war, enabled the Social Survey to develop an unparalleled expertise in survey methods. Its talented group of researchers – Louis Moss, Geoffrey Thomas, Bill Kemsley and Percy Gray in particular, who all remained with the organisation for over thirty years – transformed it into a centre skilled in sampling, questionnaire design and interviewing techniques. Moreover the range of topics covered meant that it was an exceptionally versatile instrument for helping to develop well-informed policies. Its surveys were by no means confined to social attitudes but increasingly covered factual matters such as technical advice on housing design, hospital organisation, transport problems, telephone services etc. Many of

The International Passenger Survey logo

Opposite, a nineteenth century example of survey work. Thomas Mann, Chief Clerk at the GRO in 1840, conducts a pilot survey of how much a census enumerator can do in a day (*History of Census 1841*)

the titles of its publications may sound a little bizarre, such as those on the length of cigarette stubs and on women's measurements and sizes, but they are related, in the first case, to a study of lung cancer and, in the second, to an anthropometric survey to help the clothing industry design a new series of standardised measurements for women's clothing.

Towards the end of the 1960s there were important organisational changes in government statistics, particularly social statistics. Increasing involvement by government in the day-to-day lives of people led to a need for better information and, to bring the Social Survey more into the centre of planning initiatives, it became, in 1967, a separate department responsible to a Treasury Minister. An inter-departmental committee under Treasury chairmanship was set up to advise on the programme of work. In 1970 there was a fundamental change when the Social Survey was merged with the General Register Office to form the Office of Population Censuses and Surveys.

The Social Survey Division of the Office of Population Censuses and Surveys

The merger of the two offices and the interrelationship between them was to have important implications, not only for the traditional census-taking and the registration system itself, but for the whole of social statistics. Some of the factors leading to the merger have already been described in Chapter 4 on social commentary. The practical significance for the new Office of Population Censuses and Surveys lay in the greater scope for integrating different sources of statistics. Unless information is required in detail at the local level, large-scale censuses are not necessarily the only, or even the best, way of finding out the characteristics of households or probing sensitive subjects. This can often be done more cheaply and effectively by means of smaller surveys and the transfer of the Government Social Survey into a Division within OPCS made it possible to use census and survey results to complement one another.

This possibility had already been perceived by the first Registrar General, Thomas Lister, who was given charge of the Census of Population in 1841. In 1840 he carried out what would now be described as a pilot survey to find out how much a census enumerator could do in one day. As shown in the excerpt, his chief clerk, Thomas Mann, wrote to a carefully selected number of superintendent registrars in different types of district enclosing a skeleton census form which he asked them to have completed for

It is desirable to ascertain by experiments tried in various places and under different circumstances, how much an Enumerator can do in a day; and I am to inform you that you can render an essential service by communicating with some one of the Registrars in your district and selecting with him some active and intelligent person who, in such portion of his district as you and he think it most expedient to assign, may put this question fairly to the test by going from house to house and taking down in the forms which will be supplied to him, a Census of the Population. One whole day from morning till night devoted to this work, would try the experiment most completely, and it will be proper that account should be kept of the times of commencing and finishing, and some computation made of the distance traversed. Whoever does it will of course receive remuneration.

The foregoing circular was forwarded to the Superintendent Registrars of the following selected Districts (namely):—

Westminster ; as being a densely-populated District
Birmingham
Leeds........ } as Manufacturing Districts.

Isle of Wight } as Country Districts whose Population was of
Wycomb   } average density.

Machynlleth ; as a thinly-peopled Rural District
Truro ...... ; as a Mining District.

The Superintendent Registrars of the districts referred to having expressed their readiness to assist in conducting the proposed Experiment, Skeleton Forms were prepared and printed for the purpose on loose Sheets, ruled with feint lines, and having the following headings:—

1	2	3	4		5	6
			Age and Sex			
Locality	Houses	Inhabitants	Male	Female	Occupation	Enumeration.

General Household Survey

The General Household Survey logo

the experiment. Pilot studies are commonly used in today's censuses using the facilities available in the Social Survey Division. One such example is the extensive investigation into the likelihood of getting accurate replies to an ethnic question in the census. Likewise the reliability of the census returns themselves is evaluated by follow-up surveys and the closer collaboration now possible betwen the Social Survey and Census Divisions of OPCS enables detailed checking to be carried out without breaching confidentiality.

The first major multi-purpose survey undertaken by the new office, and sponsored by the CSO, was the General Household Survey (GHS). The original plans were ambitious. They envisaged a large-scale continuous household survey which would yield quarterly data on the main social and demographic characteristics of the population and also enable ad hoc topics to be rotated in and out of the survey quickly to meet the changing needs of the government. The survey, as it finally took shape, was more modest. It was limited to 15,000 households (reduced to 12,500 in 1984) and to annual instead of quarterly analyses. The survey, which is still continuing, is carried out by interviewers who collect information about the household as a unit and also about all individual members aged 16 and over in the selected households. Those participating in the survey do so voluntarily but over 80 per cent do collaborate, so giving an effective sample today of some 10,000 households and 20,000 individuals. The main results from the survey are published in an annual report and special tabulations and tapes are also made available to government departments and private researchers.

The survey covers five 'core' subjects: population and family information, housing, employment, education and health, and it also contains a detailed section dealing with incomes. In addition, an enormously varied range of special topics is added or changed from year to year after inter-departmental discussion. In 1985, these supplementary topics included informal care of sick, elderly and handicapped persons resident in private households, dental health, private health treatment, housing tenure preferences, burglary and attempted burglary. In 1986, they included source of mortgages, interest among local authority tenants in buying their own homes and eligibility for discounts, tenure history of new owner occupiers, leisure time activities, use of day care facilities for children under five, smoking, drinking, private health insurance, and contraception, sterilisation and infertility.

A number of questions which have appeared from time to time in the Census of Population but do not need to be answered in detail on a countrywide basis are now included in the GHS. One important example is family living arrangements which now figures prominently among the questions. As a voluntary survey, the GHS has the advantage over the census in being able to investigate slightly more sensitive subjects without prejudicing the validity of the rest of the schedule.

The Labour Force Survey (LFS) is the latest household survey to be carried out by OPCS on a regular basis. All members of the European Community carry out harmonised and synchronised labour force surveys and the British one began on a biennial basis in 1973 as part of this series. It has since proved sufficiently useful for both European Community and national purposes for it to be carried out annually since 1984. For national purposes the survey has also introduced a continuing, rotating panel element of 15,000 households per quarter boosted to about 60,000 for the annual sample in the spring quarter. The first interview with a household is face-to-face but follow-up interviews in the succeeding quarters are if possible done by telephone. It is estimated that over 80 per cent of households in Britain have telephones and telephone interviewing is now used in a number of ad hoc surveys as well as for the LFS.

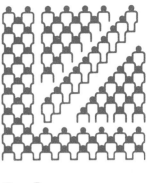

The Labour Force Survey logo

The survey schedule contains questions on personal details of household members, including nationality, country of birth and ethnic origin. It is now the most important source of information on ethnic origin. As its name suggests, however, the LFS is mainly concerned with employment and economic activity and it is the chief data source for the size of the labour force, the numbers of self-employed, hours worked, job search methods used by the unemployed, and vocational training and education. The unemployment statistics are particularly valuable as they are based on international definitions. Other countries, such as the United States, Canada, Germany and Australia, have long used the results of household surveys to calculate unemployment rates, so avoiding the deficiencies and accusations of fiddling the figures which arise from using material related to changing administrative needs and definitions, such as claimants for benefits. The main results of the survey are published in an annual report.

Although the five major surveys (NFS, FES, IPS, GHS and LFS) make up the main continuing body of work of the Social Survey Division, ad hoc surveys continue to be a very important part of its activities. Since 1970 there have been nearly 300 surveys on a wide variety of topics covering all the major areas of social and economic policy, such as health and welfare, housing, employment and labour relations, transport, financial circumstances, crime, the police and prison services and many others. There have also been major programmes of surveys on dental health, smoking and alcohol consumption and on disability, as well as a series of surveys on family planning and fertility. Many of the surveys have resulted in extensive reports and papers published by OPCS; others can be found in the published reports of Royal Commissions and Committees of Enquiry or in published articles in journals.

Until recently the Electoral Register was used as the principal source for selecting general samples for the major household surveys regularly carried out by OPCS. This has now been replaced by the Postcode Address File (PAF), and those of us who may resent having the places we live in reduced to mere numbers, may find some satisfaction in knowing that postal codes have practical uses other than just for sorting letters. The importance of a good sampling frame and sound methods in selecting samples is often not realised by those who seize upon the results of a survey without questioning too much how it has been carried out.

Many of the ad hoc surveys undertaken by OPCS are concerned with special groups of people and it is useful to be able to turn to special registers listing the sub-populations needed. The presence of the Social Survey as a division of OPCS enables it to draw on the wealth of other available sources within the Office as a whole without breaching confidentiality. For example, the samples of babies needed for the surveys of infant feeding practice carried out in 1975, 1980 and 1985 were drawn from the confidential birth registers held by another division of OPCS.

The Census of Population, also carried out by OPCS, might seem an obvious choice as a sampling frame. However, as it is taken only every ten years, the data are up-to-date for only a comparatively short time. Moreover, because filling in census forms is compulsory, the uses to which data are put can become a sensitive issue. For example, the names and addresses of a sample of persons identified from the Census of 1971 as having nursing qualifications, but who were not currently employed as nurses, were passed to the Social Survey Division for a follow-up study. Although the study was being conducted by OPCS itself, and there was therefore no breach of confidentiality, this was not generally understood and the practice was widely criticised. Accordingly, an undertaking was given at the time of the Census of 1981 that Parliament would be informed about the subject matter of any census-linked surveys which might be carried out.

Reference has already been made to the Longitudinal Study, based on a sample derived from the census, of individuals born on four specific dates in a year. The sample, first taken in 1971 and followed up in the Census of 1981, is matched with other data held by OPCS and provides a further example of the way in which data can now be brought together within the Office without breaching confidentiality.

Merging two independent organisations nearly always creates resistance, and the birth of OPCS was no exception. The result of bringing together the Government Social Survey and the General Register Office, however, has been to the benefit of both, particularly with the growing importance of sample surveys as a means of providing government with the information it needs. Private market research organisations may be cheaper and quicker and often better suited to some types of enquiry but, when quality and depth are the main criteria, the long established experience and expertise of the Social Survey Division are difficult to match. Perhaps the worst aspect of the joining of the two original bodies is the mouthful of a title with which they are now burdened!

References

1. Frank Whitehead. The Government Social Survey, in *Essays on the History of British Sociological Research*, ed. Martin Bulmer. 1985, Cambridge, CUP.

9 Health statistics: The early years of the General Register Office

Registration of deaths

The history of the GRO as described so far has been mainly concerned with the development of civil registration to meet administrative needs and of censuses and surveys for general statistical purposes. The more specific use of these sources for statistical and research requirements has been touched on only incidentally. The remaining chapters of the book continue the historical description, but also look more closely at some of the uses to which the data have been put. The present chapter, and the one which follows, is mainly concerned with the ways in which statistics have been used to help to trace the causes of sickness and death. The final chapter of the book discusses the uses of the data collected by the GRO for population research and concentrates on births, fertility and family formation.

Some of the pressure at the beginning of the nineteenth century for a reliable civil procedure for registering deaths came from the actuarial need for accurate life tables, particularly from the burgeoning number of Friendly Societies who were beginning to provide life cover, or life assurance, for the families of their members. In return for contributions this guaranteed a sum of money to a survivor on the death of the member. For this purpose the Friendly Societies therefore needed reliable information of the likely length of time a person might live at specific ages. Dr John Heysham of Carlisle had attempted to do this in the eighteenth century and from his data John Milne constructed what became known as the Carlisle life table. At the end of the century, at the request of the Equitable Society, Richard Price, a Nonconformist minister who took a keen interest in actuarial matters, computed the Northampton life table derived from parish registers and the Bills of Mortality for that city. Life tables, however, not only need

Right, William Farr writes about the history of Life tables
(*Fifth Report of the Registrar General, 1841*)

Opposite, a Northampton Bill of Mortality
(*Eighth Report of the Registrar General, 1845*)

The Life Table was invented in England by Halley the illustrious astronomer, who " first ventured to predict the return of a comet which appeared accordingly in 1759." By this simple and elegant table the mean duration of human life, uncertain as it appears to be, and as it is with reference to individuals, can be determined with the greatest accuracy in nations, or in still smaller communities. I refer to the form, and not to the mode of construction, which has been since greatly improved.

TO THE WORSHIPFUL

WILLIAM TURNER, ESQ., MAYOR,

The Aldermen, Municipal Councillors,

AND THE REST OF THE

WORTHY INHABITANTS of the TOWN of NORTHAMPTON,

This Yearly Bill of Mortality

IS PRESENTED BY THEIR MOST OBEDIENT HUMBLE SERVANT,

JOHN WRIGHT.

The Bill of Mortality

Within the Parish of All Saints, from the 21st December, 1840, to the 21st December, 1841.

DISEASES, &c., IN THE PARISH OF ALL SAINTS.

Aged . . . 19	Brain Fever . 2	Cancer . . . 1	Fits 6	Suddenly . 1
Abscess . . 2	Consumption . 28	Dropsy. . . 4	Inflammation . 19	Teeth . . 2
Apoplexy . . 1	Convulsions . 8	Drowned . . 1	Insane . . . 2	Water in the
Asthma . . 3	Croup 4	Fevers . . . 3	Measles . . 11	Head . . 4

WHEREOF HAVE DIED,

Under Two Years old 51	Ten and Twenty . 7	Forty and Fifty . 11	Seventy and Eighty. 14
Between Two & Five 13	Twenty and Thirty . 5	Fifty and Sixty . . 7	Eighty and Ninety . 2
Five and Ten . . 3	Thirty and Forty . 5	Sixty and Seventy . 2	Ninety and a Hundred 1

	CHRISTENED.			BURIED.		
	Males.	Females.	Total.	Males.	Females.	Total.
ALL SAINTS.	79	49	119	67	54	121*
ST. SEPULCHRE	49	53	102	81	62	143
ST. GILES	67	54	121	61	45	107
ST. PETER	5	10	15	9	10	19
St. John's Hospital	..	..	..	..	1	1
Independent Chapel in King Street (All Saints) . . .	..	1	1	..	6	6
Independent Meeting in St. Peter's Parish, (formerly } Doddridge's)	1	1	2	7	8	15
Baptist Meeting in College Street (All Saints); Old Bap- } tist Chapel	..	..	..	6	10	16
The Friends' Burying Ground (St. Giles).	..	..	..	..	1	1
Methodist Chapel (All Saints)	11	14	25	6	7	13
Unitarian Chapel (All Saints)	..	..	..	3	1	4
Independent, Commercial Street Chapel (All Saints) . .	3	4	7	2	5	7
Baptist Mount Zion Chapel, Newland (St. Sepulchre) . .	..	..	..	3	6	9
In the whole Town	215	177	392	245	217	462
Decrease, from last year's Bill			55	Increase	.	15

* 15 christenings and 5 interments at St. Katherine's are included in the totals of All Saints.

Is it not sweet to think, hereafter,
  When the Spirit leaves this sphere,
Love with deathless wing shall waft her
  To those she long hath mourned for here?

Hearts from which 't was death to sever,
  Eyes this world can ne'er restore,
There as warm, as bright as ever,
  Shall meet us and be lost no more?

When wearily we wander, asking
  Of earth and heaven where are they
Beneath whose smile we once lay basking
  Blest, and thinking bliss would stay?

Hope still lifts her radiant finger
  Pointing to the Eternal Home,
Upon whose portal yet they linger,
  Looking back for us to come.

Alas! alas!—doth Hope deceive us?
  Shall Friendship,—Love,—shall all those ties
That bind a moment and then leave us,
  Be found again where nothing dies?

Oh! if no other boon were given
  To keep our hearts from wrong or stain,
Who would not try to win a Heaven,
  Where all we love shall live again?

THOMAS MOORE.

SONNET.

Methought I saw the footsteps of a throne,
Which mists and vapours from mine eyes did shroud—
Nor view of who might sit thereon allowed;
But all the steps and ground about were strewn
With sights, the ruefulest that flesh and bone
E'er put on; a miserable crowd,
Sick, hale, old, young, who cried before the cloud,
"Thou art our king, O Death! to thee we groan."
Those steps I mounted, while the vapours gave
Smooth way; and I beheld the face of one
Sleeping alone within a mossy cave,
With her face up to Heaven, that seemed to have
Pleasing remembrance of a thought foregone—
A lovely Beauty in a summer grave!

WILLIAM WORDSWORTH.

* 9 buried from the parish of All Saints at the parish of St. Sepulchre, 1 ditto at the parish of St. Giles, 2 ditto at the parish of St. Peter.

accurate information on mortality by age and sex but must also be related to the age and sex of the total population. Price's tables, unfortunately, were based on deaths alone and did not take account of the changing age structure. Although he considered reasons for assuming stability the population was in fact increasing and, in such circumstances, a life table based only on mortality underestimates the expectation of life. Price's calculations did indeed do this. He estimated the average life expectancy as twenty-four years, whereas it was probably around thirty, and his Northampton table consequently had unhappy results. Not only was it widely adopted by insurance companies, but the government itself used the table when it introduced an annuity scheme as a revenue measure in 1808 and subsequently lost large sums of money[1,2].

In addition to the actuarial interest in population and mortality statistics, there was a growing realisation that accurate tracking of deaths during epidemics might help to indicate their causes and, by the 1830s, statistical analyses of death and sickness were frequently appearing in medical journals. The medical profession in particular was anxious to discover more about the causes of individual deaths and to find out ways of preventing them. In the late eighteenth century, for example, the introduction of innoculation and vaccination led to a keen interest in systematic follow-up of their effectiveness. Parliament itself, which annually voted money to the National Vaccine Establishment, founded in 1808, to promote vaccination by maintaining the supply of lymph, was also concerned that results should be monitored.

William Farr explains why Dr Price's
Northampton Life Tables were
incorrect
(*Twelfth Report of the Registrar General,
1849*)

It is shown in the paper referred to that the lifetime in Northampton was about 30 years when Dr. Price's observations were taken, whereas it is now 37½ years*; that the town contained then, as it does now, great numbers of Baptists, who repudiate infant baptism, and thus, consequently, by reducing the ratio of the christenings to the births, induced Dr. Price to believe that the population was stationary; which it is shown from other sources was, like the staple shoe trade of the place, constantly increasing.   Dr. Price assumed that the population of the parish was kept up by immigration, and that all the immigrants entered at the age of 20; as a correction for this disturbance he was induced to alter his facts, and the alteration had the effect of increasing the error of the original Table.

Dr. Price had not the data for constructing a true Northampton Table; for this reason he failed.   Dr. Price constructed from proper data a Swedish Table, which is nearly correct; and he recommended, in the first instance, his Chester Table, which is less erroneous than the Northampton Table; but the directors of the Equitable "judged it less safe."

Before the introduction of civil registration the main sources of information available on deaths were the Bills of Mortality dating back to the sixteenth century and published, with varying degrees of reliability, for a number of cities by local companies. London, for example, published weekly bills for plague deaths in 1592 and, after a lapse of a few years began publishing them again on a regular basis when plague threatened in 1603. The medical profession was increasingly aware that something more reliable was needed. Despite the advice of the various professional medical organisations, however, the original Bill in 1836 on Births and Deaths Registration did not provide for causes of death to be included in the registration procedure. Pressure from Edwin Chadwick, secretary of the Poor Law Commission at the time, and other supporters of sanitary reform persuaded the House of Lords to introduce an amendment to the Bill to enable this to be done[3].

Once the Act had been passed and civil registration set up, Thomas Lister, the first Registrar General, sent a circular to all authorised Practitioners of Medicine and Surgery in England and Wales asking them to give an authentic name of the fatal disease. His successor, George Graham, again appealed to the medical practitioners to give written statements of the cause of death and provided them with books of blank certificates for the purpose. As mentioned in Chapter 3 it was often the case that doctors did not attend people who died and the registrars were then faced with the problem of accepting what the informants told them. Often this meant just accepting the informant's guess, even if the registrar himself (as was the case in a number of districts) were a doctor. Thus, in the first few weeks of death registration for the St Peter's district of Brighton, 'decay of nature', 'decline', 'fever', 'water in the head', 'weakness', are just a few of the causes given. The Palace district records the death, on 10 July 1837 of 40 year-old Isaac Hall whilst 'indiscreetly bathing' – a picturesque description but not very helpful in establishing why or how such a person drowned.

In 1839, the GRO had the good fortune to appoint Dr William Farr as the first 'compiler of abstracts' and subsequently to promote him to 'statistical superintendent'. Farr already had a wide knowledge of vital statistics and he immediately set about improving and rationalising the available data. He remained at the GRO for over forty years, first under Thomas Lister and then under George Graham. He retired in 1880 and died a few years later, in 1883, at the age of 76.

Farr was born in 1807, the child of a farm labourer in Shropshire. At the age of two he left his parents to be adopted by

An excerpt from George Graham's circular to medical practitioners in 1845, announcing the introduction of blank Forms of Certificates for recording the cause of death.

" *may have been present at the death, or in attendance during* " *the last illness of any Person, shall immediately after such* " *death, place in the hands of such other Persons as were in* " *attendance, of the occupier of the house in which the death* " *occurred, or of some inmate who may probably be required* " *to give information, WRITTEN STATEMENTS of the* " *CAUSE OF DEATH, which such Persons may show to* " *the Registrar, and give as their information on the subject.*"

" The recommendation in this statement has been generally adopted. But it has been represented to me by Medical men engaged in practice, who take an interest in the progress of medical science, that it would save them trouble, and tend very much to promote the accuracy and uniformity of the returns, if they were supplied with blank Forms of Certificates, to be filled up by them as occasion may require.

" In compliance with this suggestion, I have requested the Registrar of the District in which you reside to supply you with a Book, which may be used when you return the Cause of the Death of any Person attended by you.

" I shall feel obliged if you will observe the suggestions in the ' Example,' on the margin of the Certificate, and in the *Statistical Nosology*, relative to the mode of making the Return.

" You are probably aware that, under 6 and 7 Wm. IV., c. 86, s. 25, the Medical attendant of the deceased person, in the last illness, is bound to give information, if applied to within eight days, with respect to the several particulars required to be registered ; but if the Cause of Death be entered by you in a Certificate, as accurately as is possible in the present state of medical knowledge, some person of the family may be the informant, give the registrar your Certificate, and save you frequent calls and inquiries.

" I need not dwell on the utility of accurate Returns of the Causes of Death, either in reference to public health, medical police, or medical science, which is based on extended observations ; but I count on your cordial co-operation and aid in obtaining from English practitioners such Registers of the important facts in question, as may promote the public good, and may deserve the imitation of the other States of Europe.

" I have the honour to be, Sir,
" Your faithful Servant,

" GEORGE GRAHAM, *Registrar General.*

" To_____

" ☞ A Copy of the ' *Statistical Nosology*' will be forwarded to you free of expense on a written application to the General Register Office, Somerset-House."

Joseph Price, the squire of the village and an elderly unmarried man who loved children. Not only did Price recognise the young boy's talents and give him a basic education but later, when he died, he left him a legacy so enabling him to become a medical student at the University of Paris and at University College, London. For a while Farr practised as a doctor in London but found it unrewarding and spent much of his time writing contributions to medical journals. He began to take a keen interest in statistics and, in 1837, published a seventy-page section on vital statistics for McCulloch's statistical digest of the British Empire: it covered a very wide range of topics and remains a classic summary of the information then available[4].

Farr's interest in mortality statistics was already apparent in the first Annual Report of the Registrar General. This report included a letter from Farr suggesting that diseases are more easily prevented than cured. The first step to their prevention is the discovery of their 'exciting causes' and 'as deaths and causes of deaths are scientific facts' they 'admit of numerical analysis':

> The deaths and causes of deaths are scientific facts which admit of numerical analysis; and science has nothing to offer more inviting in speculation than the laws of vitality, the variations of those laws in the two sexes at different ages, and the influence of civilisation, occupation, locality, seasons and other physical agencies, either in generating diseases and inducing death or in improving the public health.

In the same letter Farr argued the importance of a uniform

To be enabled to make deductions on which greater reliance may be placed, from the Causes of Death recorded in the registers, combined with the Ages and Professions of the deceased, I have considered it my duty to make an effort to induce medical practitioners to give written statements of the Cause of Death, for the purpose of registration, in all cases where fatal diseases come under their notice. I have accordingly addressed a circular letter to all the authorized practitioners throughout the country, impressing upon them the importance of attention to this matter; and I have also, at the same time, furnished them with books of blank certificates, to be filled up and placed in the hands of those persons who will be required to give information of the death to the registrar of the district in which the deceased resided.

My appeal to the medical profession has been responded to in the manner I anticipated; and I am happy to be enabled to report that, with rare exceptions, the members of that liberal and enlightened profession, now generally state in writing, for the purpose of registration, the particulars respecting the fatal diseases which come under their notice. From their exertions I hope that a correct knowledge may be obtained of the comparative prevalence of various mortal diseases, of the localities in which they respectively prevail, and the sex, age, and condition of life which each principally affects; and I trust that the Abstracts which in future years I shall be enabled to publish will form a useful addition to the records of the vital statistics of this kingdom.

The Registrar General reports on the response of the medical profession to his appeal for them to give written statements of causes of death (*Seventh Report of the Registrar General, 1843*) classification of diseases and complained that this obvious development had been given so little attention:

> Each disease has in many instances been denoted by three or four terms, and each term has been applied to as many different diseases: vague, inconvenient names have been employed, or complications have been registered instead of primary diseases.

Farr went on to replace the existing classification, first published in 1785, by a framework of his own which, with slight modifications, was still being used in the Registrar General's reports until 1880. This 'nosology', as it was then called, was circulated to medical practitioners and coroners in August 1845, with an earnest request from the Registrar General that they certify according to specified forms and avoid the use of certain 'loose or ambiguous expressions'. Despite this appeal loose phrases continued to be used and even the death, in 1867, of the distinguished Professor Michael Faraday, who admittedly died at the venerable age of 76, is described as having been due to 'decay of nature'.

A major obstacle to satisfactory reporting was that it was voluntary, and it was not until 1874 that medical practitioners were obliged to furnish to the informants, who reported the deaths to the local registrars, certificates of the causes of death of the patients they attended. In many instances of course no doctor attended either at or immediately preceding the death, and the registers of the time contain many curious descriptions reflecting the prevailing myths and beliefs of those who reported the deaths. It is perhaps of interest to note that even coroners were not always precise in their medical details. Thus, in 1858, the Swansea register, in the entry immediately preceding that of the murdered seaman in 1858 referred to in Chapter 3, records the coroner's information that the sudden death of a labourer aged 49 was due to an Act of God.

A revised list of diseases was introduced in 1881 and remained the basis of the classification used by the GRO until 1900 when, for a decade, it was replaced by a new list. In the meantime Farr's work had already prepared the way for an International Classification of Diseases (ICD) which was adopted in the United Kingdom in 1911. In 1948 the ICD was extended to enable it to be used for morbidity as well as mortality statistics and, with various revisions, it continues in use[5].

The weekly Bills of Mortality, which in many cities were the prime source of information on deaths before general registration became compulsory, did not entirely disappear when the Office was established. In London the GRO took over responsibility in 1840 by providing *Weekly Returns* of deaths and causes of deaths classified by the main entries in Farr's nosology. Gradually *Weekly Returns* were added 'for the outer Ring of London and for all the great cities in the United Kingdom'. Farr soon put the Returns to good use. For example, he noted the link between deaths from hydrophobia and rabid dogs, and he put together one set of statistics showing that, during five successive summers, no deaths in London had resulted from hydrophobia and another set of statistics showing that during these same months the police rounded up all stray dogs, particularly those suffering from rabies. From these two sets of facts he inferred that there might be a correlation or causal link. As the following extract from the twelfth Annual Report shows he expressed his thoughts in colourful language not likely to be found in today's OPCS reports:

> The causes of typhus, of cholera and the like diseases will not long . . . remain in undisturbed possession of the earth and air of this city . . . once that putrid, decaying, noisome atmosphere exhaled by churchyards, slaughter houses, the tanks of dirty water companies, cesspools, sewers and crowded dwellings is purified and dissipated.

His approach is but one example of many of the ways in which the growing body of statisticians and researchers at the GRO and elsewhere were beginning, by careful documentation, to unravel the causes of some of the diseases which beset those living in nineteenth century Britain.

Cholera

The best documented research is the identification of water supply as the chief source of cholera epidemics. There were three such major epidemics in the middle of the century – 1849, 1854 and 1866. At the GRO, Farr prepared very detailed analyses of when and where deaths occurred. With cholera, the time between onset of the disease and death is very short, averaging only some 50 hours in the 1849 epidemic. Despite the substantial additional work involved, Farr asked his staff to prepare daily totals of deaths to help identify more closely the pattern of the spread of the epidemic.

It is interesting to note that, until recently, the GRO has considered it necessary only on a few occasions to extract data on daily deaths. One such occasion was the major London fog in December 1952. Mortality increased sharply with the onset of the fog and remained high afterwards. The incident was sufficiently serious for the Minister of Health to make a special statement in Parliament and to set up a government committee to investigate the effect on health. Their report led to the passing of the Clean Air Act in 1956[6]. Recently, however, a number of studies have been using information on daily deaths. A study on infant cot deaths has been related to days of the week and research currently being conducted by the present chief medical statistician, Dr MR Alderson, relates deaths by age, sex and cause to daily temperatures.

From September 1848, as cholera approached London, Farr used the *Weekly Returns* as a news-sheet, not just for spreading

William Farr collaborated with Florence Nightingale over the collection and analysis of information on the health of the army and many other matters. The illustration shows a note to Farr from Florence Nightingale on the fly leaf of her book on lying-in institutions information, but also as a means of launching a strenuous campaign to stir the authorities into action. One of Farr's strengths was his success in working with people outside the GRO to use the information which was being collected. Just as some years later, in 1857, he began a long collaboration with Florence Nightingale to collect and analyse systematically information both on the health of the Army and many other matters, so, in 1848, he worked with Sir John Simon and Dr John Snow to identify the source of cholera infection. Sir John Simon, who had been appointed first medical officer to the City of London in 1848, used to study Farr's *Weekly Returns* of deaths in the City immediately they were published and would report on them next morning to the weekly court of the City Commission. John Snow, a distinguished·medical practitioner, used Farr's observations on the 1849 epidemic in his classic study

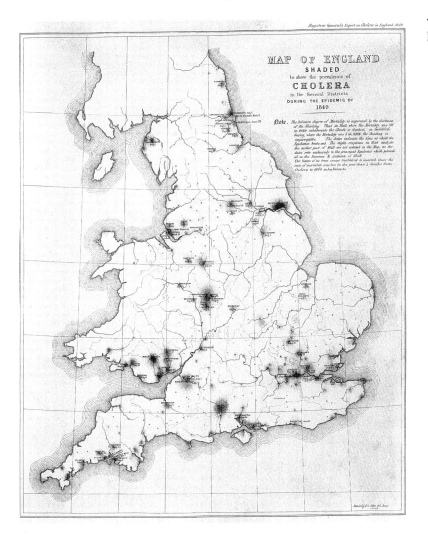

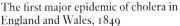

The first major epidemic of cholera in England and Wales, 1849

of cholera which anticipated the germ theory by almost twenty years. On the basis of Farr's tabulation of cholera mortality by source of water supply, he formulated his hypothesis that the cause of cholera was a self-reproducing organism excreted by victims of the disease and spread by fouled water supplies.

In the 1854 outbreak, Snow and Farr, working together, noted the occupation and residence of the victims of cholera. One such death, on 2nd September, was that of Mrs Susannah Eley who lived in Hampstead in the country outside London, an area where there were no other deaths from cholera. Farr had earlier had a theory that cholera was associated with altitude and originated from 'miasms' which, being heavier than air, tended to concentrate in those areas which were lowest and where stench from decaying matter arose most freely. According to this theory, Hampstead, being high above London, was less likely to be affected. However, by 1854 Farr had become convinced that water was the main source of the epidemic. The water in Mrs Eley's area came from the springs at Hampstead and New End and from two artesian wells and also from the New River. By chance, as a result of talking to her son, Dr Snow discovered that Mrs Eley used to send her footman daily to fetch 'pure' drinking water from the Broad Street (now known as Broadwick Street) pump next to Golden Square in the centre of the West End of London where her husband used to work. This spring was severely contaminated with cholera and, as Farr's records showed, accounted for large numbers of deaths amongst those who lived or worked in the immediate area[7].

| 439 | Second September 1854 West End | Susannah Eley | Female | 59 Years | Widow of William Eley Percussion Cap maker | Cholera Epidemica Diarrhoea 2 hours 16 hours Certified | Eliza Garaine Present at Death West End Hampstead |

Cholera in Golden Square, London: this excerpt from Dr J Snow's *On the mode of communication of cholera* describes his conversation with the son of Mrs Eley a cholera victim

I was informed by this lady's son that she had not been in the neighbourhood of Broad Street for many months. A cart went from Broad Street to West End every day, and it was the custom to take out a large bottle of the water from the pump in Broad Street, as she preferred it. The water was taken on Thursday, 31st August, and she drank of it in the evening, and also on Friday. She was seized with cholera on the evening of the latter day, and died on Saturday, as the above quotation from the register shows. A niece, who was on a visit to this lady, also drank of the water; she returned to her residence, in a high and healthy part of Islington, was attacked with cholera, and died also. There was no cholera at the time, either at West End or in the neighbourhood where the niece died.

Other statistical evidence, put together by Snow and Farr, pointed to water as the means of spreading cholera. Two different companies randomly supplied houses with piped water in a large area of south London and, by checking on cholera deaths and relating them to the source of supply, Snow's report on the 1854 outbreak showed that the ratio of deaths per 1,000 houses supplied by the two companies was as great as 14:1[8].

Farr and Snow were not alone in their campaign for better sanitation. Many voices were raised at the inactivity of the

Observations on the filth of the Thames, made in a letter by Professor Faraday to the Editor of *The Times* in 1855

SIR,

I TRAVERSED this day by steam-boat the space between London and Hungerford Bridges between half-past one and two o'clock; it was low water, and I think the tide must have been near the turn. The appearance and the smell of the water forced themselves at once on my attention. The whole of the river was an opaque pale brown fluid. In order to test the degree of opacity, I tore up some white cards into pieces, moistened them so as to make them sink easily below the surface, and then dropped some of these pieces into the water at every pier the boat came to; before they had sunk an inch below the surface they were indistinguishable, though the sun shone brightly at the time; and when the pieces fell edgeways the lower part was hidden from sight before the upper part was under water. This happened at St. Paul's Wharf, Blackfriars Bridge, Temple Wharf, Southwark Bridge, and Hungerford; and I have no doubt would have occurred further up and down the river. Near the bridges the feculence rolled up in clouds so dense that they were visible at the surface, even in water of this kind.

The smell was very bad, and common to the whole of the water; it was the same as that which now comes up from the gully-holes in the streets; the whole river was for the time a real sewer. Having just returned, from out of the country air, I was, perhaps, more affected by it than others; but I do not think I could have gone on to Lambeth or Chelsea, and I was glad to enter the streets for an atmosphere which, except near the sink-holes, I found much sweeter than that on the river.

I have thought it a duty to record these facts, that they may be brought to the attention of those who exercise power or have responsibility in relation to the condition of our river; there is nothing figurative in the words I have employed, or any approach to exaggeration; they are the simple truth. If there be sufficient authority to remove a putrescent pond from the neighbourhood of a few simple dwellings, surely the river which flows for so many miles through London ought not to be allowed to become a fermenting sewer. The condition in which I saw the Thames may perhaps be considered as exceptional, but it ought to be an impossible state, instead of which I fear it is rapidly becoming the general condition. If we neglect this subject, we cannot expect to do so with impunity; nor ought we to be surprised if, ere many years are over, a hot season give us sad proof of the folly of our carelessness.

I am, Sir,
Your obedient servant,
M. FARADAY.

Royal Institution, July 7.

responsible authorities. Charles Kingsley, who was a regular reader of the *Registrar General's Quarterly Returns*, spoke out with anger against the water companies and other vested interests whose lethargy forced people to live in filthy conditions. In a letter to his wife in 1849 he describes a visit to Bermondsey where people had nothing to drink 'but the water of the common sewer which stagnated full . . . of dead fish, cats and dogs, under their windows'. His wife, who edited his letters, describes how he worked in the crusade against dirt and bad drainage and she relates how 'The terrible revelations of the state of the Water Supply in London saddened and sickened him, and with indefatigable industry he got up statistics from Blue Books, Reports and his own observations, for an article on the subject'[9]. Professor Michael Faraday too gave his support to the campaign and in a letter to *The Times* in July 1855, likened the Thames itself to a sewer with a smell so bad that 'it was the same as that which now comes up from the gully-holes in the streets'.

Although many medical and sanitary authorities remained unconvinced by Snow even after 1854, improvements in London's water supply continued and by 1866, when cholera once more returned to England, it was all obtained from pure sources outside the city and beyond tidal waters. This time the incidence of the disease in London was light except in east London where the tally of deaths towards the end of July rose fast. The GRO's *Weekly Return* was published in *The Times* and Farr pointed an accusing finger at the East London Water Company. There were stormy scenes at Somerset House and denials from the Company, but it subsequently came to light that, because it had been a very hot summer, when the pumps threatened to run dry the East London Water Company had as an emergency measure transferred water from condemned open reservoirs near the heavily polluted tidal River Lea. Once public attention had been drawn to the issue, mortality began to decline, the implication being that the company immediately took steps to stop the polluted supply.

References

1. Glass. Op. cit.
2. John Eyler. *Victorian Social Medicine*. 1979, Baltimore and London, John Hopkins University Press.
3. Michael Alderson. William Farr's contribution to present day vital and health statistics, in *Population Trends* No. 31. 1983, London, HMSO.

4. John Eyler. Op. cit.

5. OPCS. *Population and Health Statistics in England and Wales.* 1980, London, OPCS.

6. Alison Macfarlane. Daily Deaths in Greater London, in *Population Trends* No. 5. 1976, London, HMSO.

7. A M Adelstein. Certifying Causes of Death, in *Health Trends*, Vol. 9. 1977, London; Department of Health and Social Security.

8. Fred Lewes. William Farr and Cholera, in *Population Trends* No. 31. 1983, London, HMSO.

9. Charles Kingsley. *His Letters and his Life*, ed. Mrs. F E Kingsley. 1921, London, Macmillan.

IO Health statistics: later developments

The nineteenth century

The part played by the GRO in the cholera epidemics has been described at some length not because it was the only or even the most important event in the history of the development of health statistics during the nineteenth century, but because it demonstrated very early in the life of the GRO that the registration system could be used as a powerful analytic tool and the results applied in a practical way to prevent the spread of disease. Likewise the contribution which Farr himself made to the identification of water supplies as the source of cholera infection was only a small part of his much wider achievement in developing a system of vital statistics.

At the beginning of the nineteenth century British statistics had nothing much to be proud of. Many other countries had already instituted censuses and in various European countries a great deal of information had already been put together about the health and mortality of the population. One of the most important contributions was that made by Quetelet, the Belgian philosopher and geophysicist. By the middle of the century, however, as a result of the initiative and collaboration between George Graham and William Farr, the population census in England and Wales became a model for its time, and the framework of vital statistics derived from it and from the registration system laid firm foundations for the future development of British statistics.

The work of the GRO, combined with the zeal of the sanitary reformers, played no small part in persuading Parliament that legislation could improve the health of the nation. The concluding years of Graham and Farr saw the enactment of a succession of public health measures such as the Sanitary Act of 1866 and the two Public Health Acts of 1872 and 1875. 1871 also saw the setting up of the Local Government Board which took over the powers and duties of the Poor Law Board and various functions relating to the health of the people. It remained in existence for nearly fifty years when it was replaced by the Ministry of Health in 1919. In his Annual Report for 1872, Graham commented on the confusion of responsibility which had previously prevailed at the local level and a few years later, in the 44th Annual Report for

The year 1872 will be memorable as the commencement of a new era in the promotion of health and the prevention of certain forms of disease, for one great obstacle to sanitary progress has now been removed by the passing of the Public Health Act. The confusion which existed, prior to its passing, as to who was the responsible *local* authority for sanitary purposes is to some extent removed, and a definite authority upon whom devolves the administration of the laws relating to public health is now designated.

The Registrar General comments on the first Public Health Act, 1872 (*Thirty-fifth Report of the Registrar General, 1872*)

Let us then take the entire period of ten years that elapsed between the first Public Health Act and the close of 1881. Had the death-rate remained during that period at its mean level in the preceding decade, the total deaths from 1872 to 1881 inclusively would have been 5,548,116; whereas they were actually no more than 5,155,367. Thus no less than 392,749 persons who under the old regime would have died were, as a matter of fact, still living at the close of 1881. Add to these saved lives the avoidance of at least four times as many attacks of non-fatal illness, and we have the total profits as yet received from our sanitary expenditure.

The Registrar General estimates the number of lives saved by the Public Health Acts (*Forty-fourth Report of the Registrar General, 1881*)

1881, his successor, Sir Brydges Hennicker, went so far as to make an estimate of the reduction in the number of deaths which might be attributed to the first Public Health Act.

Farr left the GRO in 1880 and died three years later. It is a tribute to the enterprise and vigour of this remarkable man that, at the age of 72 when Graham retired in 1879, he expected to become Registrar General and his disappointment at being denied the succession led to his retirement.

During the remaining years of the nineteenth century, and through into the twentieth century, the work which Farr had begun on the influence of occupation and social class assumed growing importance. Although its significance had already been appreciated by both Graham and Farr in the early days of the GRO, statistical analysis at that time had put more emphasis on the notion of 'healthy districts' as a yardstick of measurement. As early as 1841 the Registrar General's Annual Report included diagrams comparing expectation of life in different parts of the country. The 1864 report expounded once again on the evils of towns and the harm which industry brought with it. South Wales, it was said, 'has been rendered prosperous by the mines, and unhealthy by the negligence of the people'. The report then went on to warn that 'The same causes which render new works unhealthy tend to destroy the natural advantages of watering places, to which the people living in cities resort for relaxation and in search of health'.

That bad sanitation, over-crowding and poverty were some of the main factors contributing to unhealthy districts was self-evident to the social reformers of the nineteenth century. The

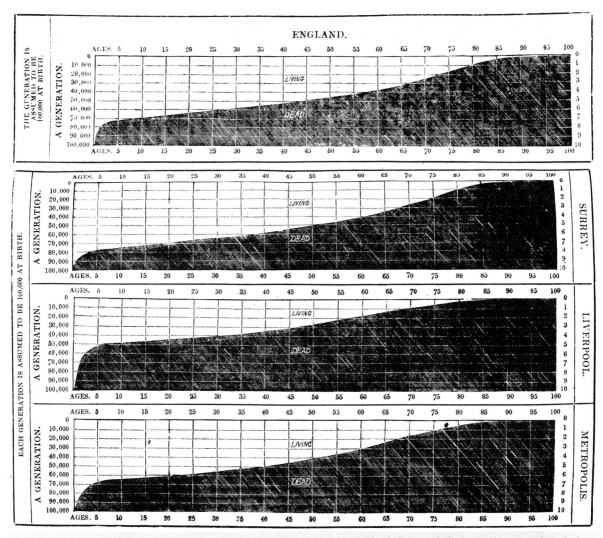

"The first diagram is intended to represent the progress of an English generation through life   the light part indicating the living, the dark the dead, at each age out of a given number (100,000) born alive.   The vertical lines divided into ten degrees serve to measure, at every fifth year, the number alive and dead at the respective ages.   The areas of the enclosed light spaces serve also to show the relative numbers living.   The second, third, and fourth, diagrams exhibit the same facts for Surrey, Liverpool, and the Metropolis.   The extent of light space upon each diagram gives a general notion of the relative population which would be maintained in the different circumstances by an *equal number* of births;

It will be seen by these Diagrams, that of the 100,000 born alive in Surrey, more than the half (50,000) are alive at the age of 50; while out of the same number born alive, 41,000 live to the age of 50 in the Metropolis, and 26,000 in Liverpool.

Comparisons of the expectation of life in different parts of the country, published in the 1841 Annual Report

association between occupation and mortality was also apparent but the link was less clear. The GRO began a systematic study of the relationship and published the results in the *Decennial Supplement on Occupational Mortality for England and Wales*. This publication first appeared in 1855, incorporating information from the 1851 Census and the mortality returns from that year, and since that time it has been published at approximately ten-yearly intervals.

Nearly all the English watering places are on good sites, and have many advantages over those abroad, and there can be no doubt that ultimately England will be the resort of foreigners who are in search of health, when we find a mortality-rate per 1000 so low as 15 in the Isle of Wight, 16 in Newton Abbot including Torquay, 17 in Cheltenham, 17 in Eastbourne, 18 in Worthing, 18 in Barnstaple, including Ilfracombe, 18 in Mutford, including Lowestoft.

The Brighton rate of mortality is 20 in 1000; but there is good reason for believing that it might be reduced to as low a rate as prevails at Cheltenham or Worthing, at a cost which would certainly be returned by its surer tenure of the public favour. Some of the seaside towns are draining their houses, and for this they deserve applause; but it appears to be very unreasonable to throw into the waters of the sea where visitors bathe the offensive matters which would fertilize the disinfecting chalk soils in the surrounding fields.

Why is the mortality of the Isle of Thanet, including Ramsgate and Margate, still 23? Why is the mortality of Hastings 24? Why is the mortality of Clifton 24? Why is it in Yarmouth at the rate of 25 in 1000?

English watering places have low mortality rates
(*Twenty-seventh Report of the Registrar General, 1864*)

Once again it was Farr who set up the method of analysis. Although occupation ('profession' or 'calling' as it was then termed) was originally included at death registration primarily as an additional identifying characteristic, Farr was quick to perceive its potential use for statistical analysis and one of his early studies related men aged 20 or more who had committed suicide in 1838 to their broad categories of occupation. In his later studies, which led to the decennial supplements, he related deaths to persons in an occupation in a time period around a census to the number of persons recorded as following that occupation in the census. Although there are obvious biases implied in using two different sources, the method has stood the test of time and is still in use today. The original pioneering work and the subsequent development of occupational mortality statistics is one of the major contributions made by the GRO to medical research. It has been a model to other countries and can claim to be without equal elsewhere.

The subsequent grouping of occupational data into social classes has already been outlined in Chapter 6 on the census, and its development is discussed further in the following chapter on

While much has been written about the diseases of shoemakers, weavers, tailors, miners, and bakers, the extraordinary mortality of butchers appears to have escaped observation. Calculation alone has taught us that the red, injected face of the butcher is an indication of a frail habit of body.

Here is an important problem for solution. On what does the great mortality of the butcher depend? On his diet, into which too much animal food and too little fruit and vegetables enter?—on his drinking to excess?—on his exposure to heat and cold?—or, which is probably the most powerful cause, on the elements of decaying matter by which he is surrounded in his slaughter-house and its vicinity?

The great mortality of the butcher
(*Fourteenth Report of the Registrar General, 1851*)

An early table of occupational mortality, published in the 1851 Annual Report

OCCUPATION.	MALES—AGES.							
	20 Years of Age and upwards.	25–	35–	45–	55–	65–	75–	85 and upwards.
	Mortality per Cent.							
Tailors - - - - - - - - -	1·998	1·163	1·415	1·674	2·818	7·647	15·528	34·737
Shoemakers - - - - - - - -	1·860	·912	1·059	1·503	2·869	6·505	16·446	34·351
Farmers and Graziers - - - - -	2·847	1·015	·864	1·199	2·490	5·530	14·802	32·379
Carpenters and Joiners - - - -	1·948	·945	1·032	1·667	2·966	6·586	14·286	33·136
Butchers - - - - - - - -	2·133	1·130	1·653	2·310	4·149	6·647	15·449	36·957
Persons engaged in the Wool, Cotton, and Silk Manufactures - - - - - -	1·777	·797	1·066	1·537	3·299	7·459	17·308	36·066
Bakers and Confectioners - - - -	1·786	·759	1·475	2·121	3·301	6·678	15·036	32·075
Inn and Hotel Keepers, Licensed Victuallers, and Beer-shop Keepers - - -	3·084	1·383	2·045	2·834	3·897	8·151	18·084	40·860
Grocers - - - - - - - -	1·519	·763	1·046	1·579	2·265	4·972	12·457	19·231
Miners, &c., viz. Coal, Iron, Copper, Tin, and Lead Miners; Persons engaged in Iron, Copper, and Lead Manufactures; Workers and Dealers in Copper, Tin, and Lead -	1·511	·849	1·135	2·015	3·450	8·051	17·867	23·179
Labourers, &c., viz. Agricultural Labourers, Farm Servants, and Shepherds; General Labourers, Railway Labourers, and Navvies; Stone, Slate, and Limestone Quarriers, and other Workers in Stone and Clay; Bricklayers and Marble Masons -	2·163	·979	1·252	1·730	2·920	6·790	17·394	41·795
Blacksmith - - - - - - - -	1·854	·812	1·240	1·651	3·724	7·443	16·710	33·133
All MALES aged 20 Years and upwards in England - - - - - -	2·009	·948	1·236	1·787	3·031	6·396	14·055	28·797

population. During the present century it has had and continues to have a profound influence on statistical analysis. For example, a committee set up by the Secretary of State for the Department of Health and Social Security in 1977, was asked to look at the differences in health status amongst the different social classes and to suggest possible causal factors and their implications for policy. The report, which came to be known as 'The Black Report' (from the name of its chairman, Sir Douglas Black), stated that the committee had largely had to use occupational status as an indicator of social equality because few other indicators were available. It considered that for the population in general, though not for many groups at particular health risk such as the elderly retired, the classification reasonably reflected such other aspects of social inequality as differences in financial resources, housing and education. One of its main conclusions was that the health experience of the unskilled and semi-skilled manual classes relative to Social Class I had not improved during the 1960s and early 1970s, and in some respects had declined. The difference in infant mortality between the lowest and the highest classes increased between 1959–63 and 1970–72. The committee was also concerned about the inequalities which existed in the use of the health services, particularly the preventive services. An extract from the committee's conclusions is shown (above opposite).

Most recent data show marked differences in mortality rates between the occupational classes, for both sexes and at all ages. At birth and in the first month of life, twice as many babies of "unskilled manual" parents (class V) die as do babies of professional class parents (class I) and in the next 11 months 4 times as many girls and 5 times as many boys. In later childhood the ratio of deaths in class V to deaths in class I falls to 1.5–2.0, but increases again in early adultlife, before falling again in middle and old age. A class gradient can be observed for most causes of death, being particularly steep in the case of diseases of the respiratory system. Available data on chronic sickness tend to parallel those on mortality. Thus self-reported rates of long-standing illness (as defined in the General Household Survey) are twice as high among unskilled manual males and 2½ times as high among their wives as among the professional classes. In the case of acute sickness (short-term ill health, also as defined in the General Household Survey) the gradients are less clear.

Social class differences in health. An extract from the Black Report on *Inequalities in Health* (1980)

Vaccination in the nineteenth century

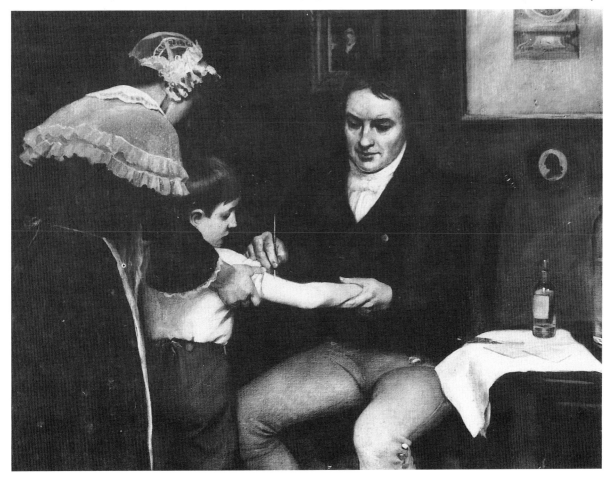

Although infant mortality remained high until the end of the nineteenth century expectation of life at most ages increased gradually, particularly during the second half of the century. The fall in death rates was almost entirely due to the decrease in infectious diseases and the less virulent form which some of them took. There is little doubt that better sanitation, cleaner water supplies and improved nutrition were primarily responsible, and that increasing medical knowledge played only a small part. There were however certain landmarks in the medical and legislative field. Vaccination against smallpox became compulsory in 1853. Antiseptics and anaesthetics in surgery were beginning to be used in the middle of the century, and Dr John Snow administered chloroform to Queen Victoria in 1853 at the birth of Prince Leopold, her eighth confinement. Notification of infectious diseases became compulsory in 1895. Many of the main hospitals in the big cities had already been built in the eighteenth century, but the important contribution which the training of nurses made to the health of the patients had to wait until Florence Nightingale set the example by founding a nurses training school at St Thomas's Hospital in London in 1861.

The twentieth century

Since the nineteenth century the pattern of disease has changed and most of the infectious epidemics which were then prevalent now belong to history. With the exception of tuberculosis which was not conquered until the 1940s, the epidemics which have so far been of most concern in the twentieth century have been mainly chronic diseases, such as coronary thrombosis or cancer of the lung. The statistics needed to study these diseases and the type of research carried out have reflected the change. Moreover the administrative structure of the country is now quite different from the days when the GRO was first established and it has brought with it a whole new range of statistics about death and disease. Today's computers enable us to store this vastly increased information and analyse it more intensively.

The death certificate and the population census remain essential sources for medical research but they have been supplemented with, for example, data collected from hospitals since 1949 about the illness of their patients (the Hospital In-Patient Enquiry), information on accidents collected by a variety of departments, National Insurance records and the Central Register of patients maintained for the National Health Service.

More recently, further legislation on notification has resulted in additional statistics on other medical conditions. Partly arising from anxiety about the harmful effects of radiation, the 1960 Population (Statistics) Act required compulsory notification of the causes of still-births. The thalidomide tragedy in 1960 was an important factor leading to the setting up, in 1964, of a national scheme for notifying congenital abnormalities. In 1968, when abortion was legalised, each pregnancy terminated has had to be notified together with information on the associated circumstances.

The NHSCR is a particularly important source of information. Local NHS registers are held by the ninety eight family practitioner committees (FPCs) who are responsible for paying doctors on a 'capitation' basis related to the age of their patients. The NHSCR helps these FPCs by acting as a clearing house for passing on information on transfers between doctors, controlling the issue of new NHS numbers and ensuring that FPCs are notified when people no longer need NHS care because they have, for example, gone abroad, joined the Forces or died. The Central Register is also annotated with a cipher for each person registered with cancer.

The origin of the NHS numbers of those living in England and Wales in 1939 was the national registration number allocated to them shortly after the outbreak of war (see Chapter 7). Because of the length of time it has been in existence, the National Register is now an important data source. It contains the names, ages and addresses of those registered in 1939 and, through the NHSCR which includes everyone registered with a doctor, can be used to trace the subsequent mortality of people living in particular areas in 1939.

In addition to statistics derived from administrative sources, special surveys are also an important data source. During the Second World War the need to keep a watch over the effect of the 'black-out', bombing and long hours of work on the nation's health, led to the Survey of Sickness. This important continuing survey of morbidity and the use of medical services was carried out on behalf of the GRO by the Wartime Social Survey. Its instigator was Dr Percy Stocks, who had succeeded Dr Stevenson in 1933 as the Registrar General's chief medical statistician. Information was collected by interviewing samples of the adult civilian population each month about their health in the previous two to three months. From 1944 until 1952 the Survey was published regularly in the *Registrar General's Quarterly Return*, and the information was used to throw light on a number of specific problems relating to sickness and incapacity. A little later, in 1955–56, a National Morbidity Survey based on medical records kept by doctors in a sample of general practices was conducted by the GRO in conjunction with the Royal College of General Practitioners. Similar studies were carried out in 1970–71 and 1981–82. 1971 saw the start of the annual General Household Survey which includes questions about the health of individuals in their household setting.

Special surveys designed to monitor specific diseases have been widely used and, as mentioned earlier, the Social Survey Division of OPCS has carried out innumerable studies related to smoking, drinking, dental health, disability, long term disablement, infant feeding and so on. A recent study of a sample of inner London patients is designed to link their records with deaths reported to the NHSCR and to compare the mortality of those who were incapacitated at the time of the survey with those who were not.

This linking of surveys with administrative data, such as the NHSCR, held by OPCS is an important development in research. The main linkage study, already referred to in Chapter 7 on the census, is the Longitudinal Study linking a sample of individuals from census to census and to records kept in the registration system. The study was started in 1971, as part of the census operation, and consists of a one per cent sample of the population drawn from all individuals born on four selected dates in any year. It is updated by adding to it subsequent births and immigrants born on these dates and deducting from it deaths and study members who emigrated. These events are identified from the NHSCR and are notified to those in charge of the study.

Medical research concerned with identifying the causes of many of the chronic diseases afflicting present society often depends on linking different data sources, particularly registration information and its transfer to the NHSCR. For example, linkage of birth registration data to infant death details was carried out as a special study for infants born in 1949–50 and again for 1964–65: from 1975 it has become a regular study. By following up subsequent histories in the NHSCR recent studies have examined the pattern of mortality of those known to have been exposed to asbestos dust or to have consumed high levels of alcohol.

Trends in mortality

The published statistics of the GRO provide a series of annual death rates extending back 150 years to 1837. Changes of one kind or another over this period, such as revisions of the International Classification of Diseases, however make it difficult to interpret the underlying causes which contribute to the overall figures. Not only have there been changes in the way the facts have been collected and presented, but the meanings of the terms used have themselves altered. It was not until 1874 that death registration had to be accompanied by a certificate from the doctor last in attendance on the deceased, and it was only gradually during the second half of the century that vague terms such as old age, dropsy, convulsions and natural causes ceased to be accepted by the registrars. It was 1940 before fuller and more systematic information on underlying causes of death was included. But even today medical terminology and classification is not a precise matter. Certificates are completed by doctors of varying experience – about half by hospital doctors, a quarter by GPs and a quarter by coroners; in only one third of deaths has there been a post-mortem examination.

Apart from these problems there are changing fashions in medical certification so that it can be difficult to decide whether apparent increases in particular causes of death reflect a real increase in incidence or merely a new attitude to certification. Better diagnostic facilities have added to the difficulties. A typical example in recent years is the increasing number of deaths due to disease of the coronary arteries. It is possible that among some groups of people this cause went undiagnosed in earlier periods, and that it was the better access to doctors by the more wealthy which led to their being diagnosed as suffering from heart disease and hence to the acceptance of it as a 'disease of affluence' in the 1930s[2].

When the population composition of a country is changing, those causes of death which affect different age-groups will also

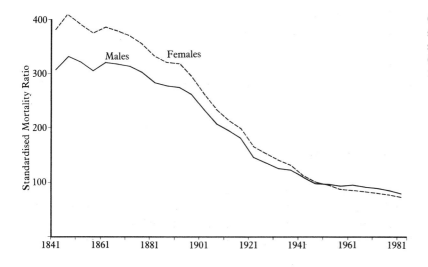

Chart 10.1 Mortality ratios, standardised to relate to the age structure of the population in 1950–52 (= 100) England and Wales, 1841 to 1985

influence the overall death rate. Thus, when the population is ageing, as in England and Wales today, the causes of death which affect the elderly become more important: this can mean that, even if there is no change in life expectation over the life span, the average, or crude, death rate will probably be higher at the end than at the beginning of a period. One way of making some allowance for this effect is to use standardised rates which reflect age changes in the population. Chart 10.1, which gives standardised death rates for the total population from 1841 to the present day, shows that during the first forty years of the GRO, which coincided with the active professional career of Dr Farr, mortality rates remained virtually unchanged. During the rest of the century, however, public health reforms, improved housing and rising standards of living, despite the agricultural and industrial depression in the 1880s, were reflected in marked falls in death rates. The significant exception was infant and child mortality (Chart 10.2), which showed no improvement until the beginning of the next century. In the early years of the twentieth century mortality rates for the total population continued to fall in response to improvements in social conditions and increasing medical attention, particularly personal health services such as maternity and child welfare clinics, health visiting and medical inspection in schools. It was not until the 1930s however that major advances in medical practice and in drug use, particularly sulphonamides in the late 1930s, penicillin in the early 1940s and other antibiotics in the post-war years, became a substantial factor in reducing death rates.

Chart 10.3 and Table 10.1, for the years 1848–72, 1901–10 and 1981–85, are based for the first two time-periods on a study by W P D Logan who was Chief Medical Officer at the GRO from 1951 to 1961. For the reasons already explained, comparisons

Chart 10.2   Infant and childhood mortality, England and Wales, 1846–1985

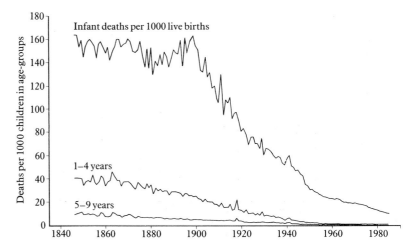

	1848–72	1901–10	1981–85
All causes	**1000**	**1000**	**1000**
Infectious diseases	321	200	3
of which:			
tuberculosis	146	84	1
typhoid and typhus	38	7	–
smallpox	13	1	–
measles	19	20	–
scarlet fever	57	7	–
diphtheria	na	11	–
whooping cough	20	16	–
influenza	3	13	–
cholera	10	–	–
Cancer	9	47	199
Diseases of the nervous system	129	117	12
Heart diseases	37	86	390
Bronchitis	66	72	28
Pneumonia	57	90	49

Rates of less than 0.5 are represented by a dash (–)

Table 10.1   Proportional rates for selected diseases per 1000 deaths from all causes – males, England and Wales. (Source: Logan[3] and OPCS.)

Chart 10.3   Mortality of males from selected causes of death, England and Wales, 1848–72, 1901–10 and 1981–85 (Source: Logan[3] and OPCS.)

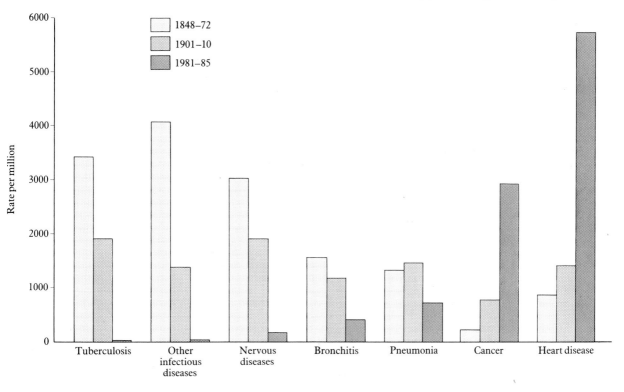

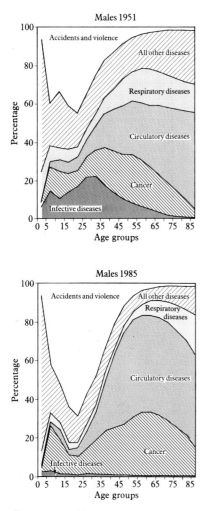

Males 1951

Accidents and violence
All other diseases
Respiratory diseases
Circulatory diseases
Cancer
Infective diseases

Males 1985

Accidents and violence
All other diseases
Respiratory diseases
Circulatory diseases
Cancer
Infective diseases

Chart 10.4   Above and opposite, selected causes of death by age and sex, England and Wales, 1951 and 1985

between periods over such a long period of time cannot be precise, but they suffice to show the broad trend of changes in the causes of death of males. In the early days of the GRO one death in every three was attributed to infectious diseases. Within this group the highest individual cause was respiratory tuberculosis, accounting for approximately one third of all deaths from infectious diseases, followed by scarlet fever and diphtheria (not separately distinguished in the records until 1855). By the turn of the century infectious diseases amongst males accounted for only one death in five and by 1981–85 they were insignificant. All the individual infectious diseases except influenza contributed to this reduction. Cholera and typhus entirely and smallpox and typhoid all but disappeared. Scarlet fever became a mild disease and in response to immunisation campaigns diphtheria and other childhood infections became relatively unimportant.

In contrast to infectious diseases, chronic diseases, such as cancer and heart diseases, have become increasingly important causes of death in the present century. The incidence of heart diseases, which now account for about a quarter of all deaths of women and nearly one third of men, take a particularly severe toll of men in the middle years of life. Cancer on the other hand is the major cause of death for women at these ages.

Conclusion

In the early years of the GRO the range of statistics developed and the analysis and research carried out played a significant part in identifying the pattern of disease and tracing its causes. The reports of the Registrar General used the regular returns and reports of the GRO to draw attention to the state of the nation's health and social conditions, and these in their turn helped to shape government policy and reform public health. After the improvements which followed sanitary reform in the latter half of the nineteenth century the emphasis of the reports and the nature of the predominating diseases shifted. In the present century the growth of State participation and provision of services has brought with it a greatly increased range of statistics derived from administrative sources, and the linking of some of these within OPCS to registration and census information has opened up the range of uses and applications of the data. The twentieth century has also seen the appointment, in 1919, of a Minister of Health who now publishes the report prepared by the Government's Chief Medical Officer of Health. These reports on the 'State of the

Public Health' in England, have been submitted every year since Dr (later Sir) John Simon was appointed Medical Officer to the Privy Council in 1856. Much of the information in the reports, however, is based on data collected by OPCS and depends on close collaboration between the two Departments.

References

1. *Cancer Incidence and Mortality in the Vicinity of Nuclear Installations, England and Wales, 1959–1980.* SMPS 51, 1987, London, HMSO.

2. Mildred Blaxter. Fifty Years On – Inequalities in Health, in *British Society for Population Studies Conference Papers*, University of East Anglia, 1986.

3. W P D Logan. Mortality in England and Wales from 1848–1947, in *Population Studies*, Vol. IV, 1950–51.

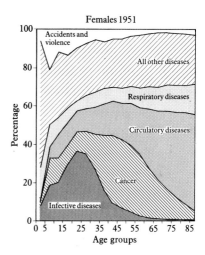

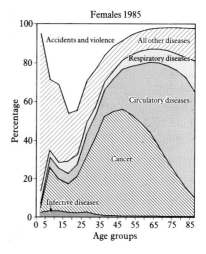

II Population

Before 1800

The first Census of Population in 1801 gave the total number of people in England and Wales as nine million. Some of the events which led up to Parliament's decision to hold a census have been discussed in earlier chapters. One of the more important was that other countries had found it necessary, for practical and administrative purposes, to take censuses. On introducing the Population Bill into the House of Commons, Charles Abbot remarked that it had 'long been a matter of surprise and astonishment, that a great and powerful nation like this should have remained hitherto unacquainted with the state of the population.' He went on to say:

> But, Sir, in times like these when the subsistence of the people is in question, this knowledge becomes of the highest importance. It is surely important to know the extent of the demand for which were are to provide a supply: and we should set about obtaining it immediately. . . .

In England and Wales there had been a continuing controversy about the size of the population. Various estimates had been made and there was considerable debate about whether it was decreasing or increasing. There was concern lest the population might be outstripping the capacity to produce sufficient food and these fears were increased by the bad harvest of 1800. As David Glass writes, 'Concern with the increasing burden of the poor, and with the need to import food, began to erode the earlier mercantilist belief in the advantages of a large and increasing population, and the new views were crystallized by Malthus.'[1] When the GRO was set up in 1837 to administer the registration service, a further and more accurate source of statistics on year-to-year changes between censuses then became available. These events have been described in earlier chapters and this concluding chapter now looks at the broad changes in population, both before and after 1837, and at some of the factors which lay behind them.

Demographers have tried to reconstruct the early trends, both in total population and in fertility and mortality. The most recent research, for England only, is that by E A Wrigley and R S

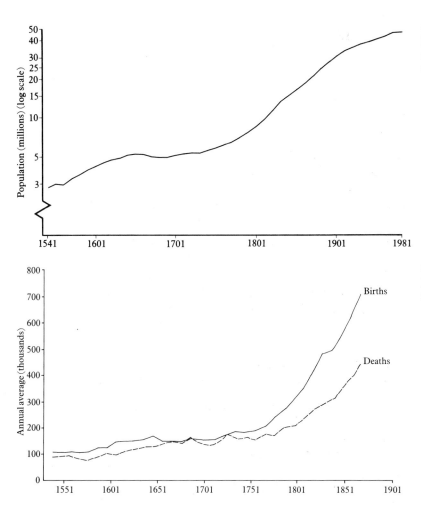

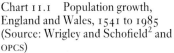

Chart 11.1   Population growth,
England and Wales, 1541 to 1985
(Source: Wrigley and Schofield[2] and
OPCS)

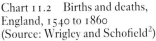

Chart 11.2   Births and deaths,
England, 1540 to 1860
(Source: Wrigley and Schofield[2])

Schofield for the period 1541–1871, and charts based on their
work have been included to give a general perspective to more
recent trends[2]. Chart 11.1 shows that population, after being stable
at about five million people for a hundred years from the middle of
the seventeenth to the middle of the eighteenth century, began to
increase quite sharply. The rise, as indicated in Charts 11.2, 11.3
and 11.4, was mainly due to an increasing number of births and
higher fertility. Death rates were also decreasing and expectation
of life was rising. It is interesting to note that the estimates
published by Wrigley and Schofield suggest that expectation of life
at birth from 1566 to 1621, during the reigns of Elizabeth I and
James I, was probably remarkably high, reaching a peak of nearly
42 years in 1581 and averaging over 38 years for the period as a
whole. Thereafter it fell and did not pick up again until well into
the eighteenth century. The available estimates suggest that it was
not until 1871 that the previous record in 1581 was surpassed.

Chart 11.3   Expectation of life, England, 1551 to 1861 (five-year moving averages) (Source: Wrigley and Schofield[2])

Chart 11.4   Gross reproduction rate, England, 1551 to 1861 (five-year moving averages) (Source: Wrigley and Schofield[2])

Although a high level of emigration was considered desirable in order to populate British overseas possessions, there was some concern lest the population was being unduly depleted by colonisation. This was a further reason for the growing interest in finding out the facts. Firm figures are hard to come by but, in the two and a half centuries before 1800, Wrigley and Schofield have suggested that the net loss was low compared with the surplus of births over deaths and hence did not play a significant part in population change. At particular periods, however, such as between the mid seventeenth and mid eighteenth centuries when a large number of people left England and when the natural increase may have been small or even negative, it had a more powerful influence on population growth[3].

The importance of fertility in estimating population

In the first half of the nineteenth century the population was growing fast. Many people, including the Registrar General, brushed aside Malthus's gloomy prognostications and accepted this as part of Britain's greatness. In the Registrar General's report for 1840–41 Graham noted that the population had increased in geometrical progression, but he saw no reason why resources should not increase at the same rate and enhance the greatness and prosperity of the country. Nor did he see why there should be any slackening 'in the zeal of some in ameliorating the public health' for fear that an excess population might increase human misery. Moreover, his faith was such that he believed equilibrium between subsistence and population would somehow be safeguarded by God and the laws.

During the early years of the GRO, as the previous chapters have indicated, there was much greater emphasis on getting to know more about deaths than about births. For example, registration of a death included age of the deceased as well as sex, occupation and cause of death. Used together with the information from the census on the age distribution of the population it became possible to compile detailed life tables and enabled Farr to develop one of the most sophisticated systems of the time for estimating and measuring mortality. The emphasis on mortality was understandable. Initially the emergence of life insurance had resulted in the need for accurate mortality statistics, but it was also generally believed that mortality was the major factor influencing population growth and that fertility was a constant determined only by the number of marriages.

....The population, it has been proved, has increased in a geometrical progression ever since the first census in 1801 : and the rate of progression has been such that, if it continue, the numbers will have doubled in 1850 : double the number of families will exist, and must be supplied with subsistence in England : but there will also be double the number of men to create subsistence and capital for her families, to man her fleets, to defend her inviolate hearths, to work the mines and manufactories, to extend the commerce, to open new regions of colonization ; and double the number of minds to discover new truths, to confer the benefits and to enjoy the felicity of which human nature is susceptible. If the proposition of Lord Bacon be sound, as it unquestionably is, that the "true greatness (of a state) consisteth essentially in population and breed of men," time has confirmed his prescient assertion, "that out of doubt none of the great monarchies, which in the memory of time have risen in the habitable world, had so fair seeds and beginning as hath this estate and kingdom."....

The true greatness of a State
(*Fourth Report of the Registrar General, 1840*)

In contrast to the detailed information collected on deaths, much less attention was given to the trends in marriage or fertility. Birth certificates included the date of birth, the child's and the parents' names and the occupation of the father, but gave no information on the age of the mother. Statistics therefore could not be compiled about births to women at specific ages during their reproductive lives but could only be related to measures such as the total population and the number of marriages. Furthermore, because it was not compulsory (until 1874) for parents to register a birth unless requested to do so by the registrar, the registers were known to be deficient, particularly in the early years after 1837. Marriage registration was also often unsatisfactory. Most marriages involved religious ceremonies and, as recording by the clergy was less thorough than that by registrars, the information on occupation and ages tended to be poor.

When civil registration was introduced in Scotland in 1855, much more information was from the start included on births than in England and Wales. This enabled Dr J Matthews Duncan to carry out a very detailed study of the fertility of women which he published in 1866 under the title of 'Fecundity, Fertility, Sterility and Allied Topics.' He comments in his introduction that '. . . in consequence, I believe, of numerous complaints regarding the irksome labour of filling up the document it was discontinued, and a much less comprehensive schedule has been in use ever since.'[4].

Interest in fertility in England and Wales developed much later. This was partly because it was thought that families, and women in particular, might be sensitive about disclosing information on length of marriage and numbers of children born and still alive. But equally important was the belief, held by the social reformers of the time, that intervention by government to improve public health and conditions could prevent death and disease but could have little impact on fertility. Nor were they particularly concerned about the number of births. Their attitude was that if births were substantially exceeding deaths, then why worry. As the Registrar General himself said in his Annual Report for 1904, 'so long as the fall in the birth rate in this country continues to be balanced by reduced mortality, there would hardly appear to be serious cause for alarm'. It was not until much later in the century,

The high level of infant mortality causes concern
(*Sixty-seventh Report of the Registrar General, 1904*)

In view . . . of the fact that little can probably be done by legislation to arrest the increasing decline in the birth-rate, it is no doubt of paramount importance that effective measures should be devised to lessen the enormous death-roll caused by "Infant Mortality." This should be regarded as one of the master-keys to the situation.

> ... the number of births depends in the first place upon the number of men and women between certain ages. For practical purposes the ages of twenty and forty are sufficiently near the mark, and they are much more convenient than the ages for each sex which would have to be taken if perfect accuracy were required. Now from 1853 to 1876 the number of births, after allowing for some deficiency in registration, increased rapidly and was almost uniformly just about 12 per cent on the number of persons between twenty and forty. From 1876 onwards the number of births has been almost stationary, and the rate per cent on the persons between twenty and forty has consequently been rapidly declining. In ten years it had fallen to 11 per cent; by 1890 it had further fallen to 10 per cent; in 1891 it went up to about 10.4 per cent; in the next two years it was 10 per cent; in 1894 it descended to 9.8 per cent.

Edwin Cannan discusses fertility
(*The Economic Journal*, 1895)

when it was becoming clear that the birth rate was falling quite steeply, that fertility – and infant mortality – attracted attention and concern began to be voiced outside the GRO by people such as Edwin Cannan and the eugenists.

At the end of the century it also became evident that the fall in the birth rate and the effect it would have on the size of future generations of women of childbearing age could, in the next century, lead to a fall in population. The Registrar General had already been making intercensal population estimates since the middle of the century, at first for England and Wales only but later for all registration counties and for most major large towns and districts, but these estimates were prepared by extrapolating from the two preceding censuses and took no account of changing trends in the component factors.

This approach was sharply criticised by Edwin Cannan in an article in the December 1895 issue of *The Economic Journal* (vol. 5 no. 20) where he wrote that population estimates ought to take account separately of births, deaths and net migration. He went on to say that 'in estimating future population the most important data we have to rely upon are the ages of the people as taken at recent censuses'. He had noted that the birth rate had been falling and that 'the statistics make it probable that the birth rate of persons between twenty and forty will continue to fall.' Each successive

> The truth is that every estimate of population, past, present, and to come, ought to be founded on a consideration of the factors on which the growth or decline of population is dependent–births, deaths, immigration, and emigration. The number of births and deaths, and of immigrants and emigrants, is now so well known, that if two government departments, the Board of Trade and the General Registry Office, would only recognise each other's existence, the population at the present time, or at any point in recent years, could be given within ten thousand of the actual number.

Estimating the population
(Edwin Cannan, *The Economic Journal*, 1895)

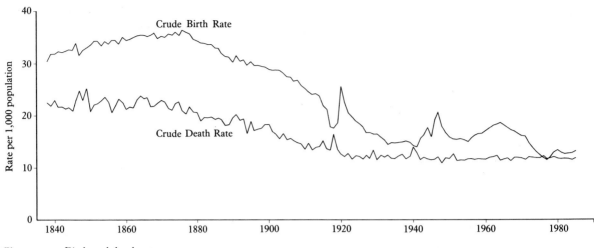

Chart 11.5   Birth and death rates,
England and Wales, 1837 to 1985

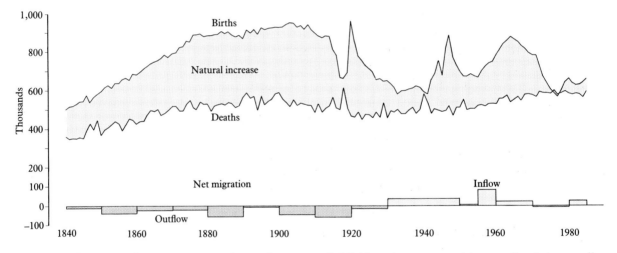

Chart 11.6   Population changes,
England and Wales, 1841 to 1985

cohort of women of child bearing age would accordingly be smaller than the previous one. Given the assumption of no change in mortality and no net loss by migration, the question to be answered therefore was the probable number of births. His conclusion was that population growth would cease in the twentieth century. As it was still growing by well over 10 per cent per decade this at the time seemed unlikely. Although his precise predictions were not particularly accurate—by 1916 the population had already increased beyond his estimate of the maximum it would ever reach—Cannan did identify the factors which have since led to a marked slowing down of growth and his approach to forecasting was an important development in demographic analysis[5].

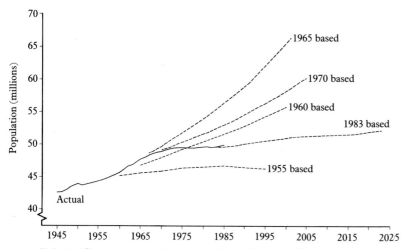

Chart 11.7 Projected population of England and Wales

Edwin Cannan had also perceived that predicting births was and still remains the most difficult problem. Today's population projections for Great Britain as a whole are carried out by the Government Actuary's Department in consultation with the Registrars General of England and Wales and of Scotland, and their actuaries and statisticians are the first to admit that attempts to project, or make assumptions about, the many still only partly understood social and demographic variables which lie behind family-building decisions are fraught with pitfalls. Population projections are based on what are believed to reflect the most recent underlying trends but, as demonstrated by the diagram giving the latest projections for total population set against earlier ones made over the last 30 years (Chart 11.7), the projected figures can be very different to what actually happens. In a recent paper for the British Society for Population Studies, Professor Grebenik concluded with the following comment:

> But as regards an understanding of the fundamental factors which motivate individual reproductive behaviour, I find myself after nearly 50 years in the trade in the position of Goethe's Faust
> > 'And here I stand with all my lore
> > Poor fool no wiser than before'[6]

Falling birth rates

The pronounced fall in birth rates at the end of the nineteenth century was as disturbing to many people as the rise had been to Malthus a century earlier, particularly as fertility was relatively low amongst the upper and middle classes, and a growing understanding of the laws of heredity led to anxiety lest the quality of the population should deteriorate.

An upper class gentleman replies to a question on the state of families in 1874
(C Ansell, *Statistics of families in the Upper and Professional classes*, 1874)

" *There will be no more.*"
Hoorah!

One gentleman after stating, evidently with all due regard to correctness, the particulars of his somewhat numerous offspring, winds up with the accompanying graphical illustration of his satisfaction at there being no prospect of a further increase in their number.

The debate concerning the possible decline in the quality of the population was fuelled by the soul-searching over the issue of national efficiency following the reverses of the second Boer War at the turn of the century. There were those who believed that inherited natural characteristics were responsible for a deterioration in national intellect and physique, and that this was caused by the misguided humanitarianism of the Public Health movement which attempted to curb mortality and morbidity by preventive health measures of hygiene and sanitation. This concern was reflected in 1908 in the formation of the Eugenics Education Society with Sir Francis Galton, cousin of Charles Darwin, as president. He was an anthropologist who applied statistical methods to the study of human characteristics and he and the Society were to have a strong influence on demographers during the first part of the twentieth century.

At the beginning of the century, as a result of the initiative of the Registrar General, Sir Bernard Mallet, and his statistical superintendent, Thomas Stevenson, questions relating to the fertility of married women were included in the 1911 Census of Population. These questions asked about the length of marriage and the number of living children born to each marriage, the number still living and the number who had died; they were addressed to married women only, so any widows or single women who had had children were omitted. It was thought that women would be embarrassed to answer the question on the number of children but, in the event, there seems to have been no problem. The use of punch cards for processing the results helped considerably in the sophisticated analysis required, but unfortunately the analysis was held up by the war which diverted GRO staff to other matters and the first part of the report was not published until 1917 with the second part being delayed until 1923.

Against the background of the 'Nature versus Nurture' controversy, Stevenson set about trying to establish the facts and considered very carefully the influence of social class on both

Table 11.1 Total fertility of marriages in various classes at various dates, as measured by total births, and expressed as a per cent of the corresponding rate for all classes jointly. 1911. England and Wales

Date of Marriage	Upper and Middle Class	Higher Inter- mediate Class	Skilled Work- men	Lower Inter- mediate Class	Un- skilled Work- men	Textile Workers	Miners	Agri- cultural Labourers
1851–61	89	99	101	99	103	94	108	105
1886–91	74	87	100	101	112	90	126	114
1891–96	74	88	99	101	113	88	127	115
1896–1901	76	89	99	101	114	86	125	114

Source: Stevenson. Paper given to Royal Statistical Society on The fertility of various social classes from the middle of the nineteenth century to 1911. April 1920

We were already well aware that the more successful and prosperous classes were behindhand in their contribution to the upkeep of the nation; but it was possible to suppose that this might long have been the case, and that, therefore, experience had proved it to be compatible with such prosperity and advancement as had been achieved. Now, however, this comforting view is no longer tenable. In the deficient fertility of the classes which, having achieved most success in life, are presumably best endowed with the qualifications for its achievement, we see that we have to face a new and formidable fact—how formidable is a question which must be left for the consideration of authorities on eugenics.

Stevenson's analysis of fertility shows that the more successful and prosperous classes have smaller families
(The fertility of various social classes from the middle of the nineteenth century to 1911, Journal of the Royal Statistical Society April 1920)

fertility and infant mortality. As already described in Chapter 6, the first reference to the social class gradings which have subsequently become such an important influence on social research, was in the Registrar General's Annual Report for 1911, and they were also used for the analysis of the 1911 Census. The first analyses in the 1911 Census separated out textile workers, miners and agricultural labourers as being worthy of separate study but they were reallocated between the five main classes at the time of the 1921 Census. Table 11.1 is derived from a paper which Stevenson gave to the Royal Statistical Society in 1920. He drew attention not only to the marked class differential in fertility but also to the widening gap between the classes over the years corresponding, so he surmised, to the spread of contraceptive practice. In his paper he also noted the effect of employment on women's fertility and concluded that occupied mothers had exceptionally low fertility.

Despite the increasing concern about the possibility that population growth in England and Wales might cease, the GRO for the most part remained aloof. Although Sir Bernard Mallet,

Registrar General from 1909 to 1920, attended the first World Conference on Population held in Geneva in 1927, there was no one else present who was currently on the staff of the GRO. This reflected the comparative lack of interest by the Office in population questions at this time. During the 1930s, when it was fairly clear that fertility was well below replacement level, it was not possible to calculate fertility rates specific by age or duration of marriage because this required more detailed data than was available from the existing statistics. These rates could only be estimated. Sir Sylvanus Vivian, the Registrar General at the time, agreed to take steps to obtain information about the ages of the parents and date of marriage when a birth was registered, but reform was delayed by a belief that individual privacy would be breached. Indeed, the official attitude, perhaps in keeping with the philosophy of the time that government intervention in the lives of the people should be kept to a minimum, was that no action was necessary and that public concern about the declining birth rate was excessive and exaggerated[7].

The universitites, too, had given little attention to population studies, but it was the academic world, in conjunction with the Eugenics Society, which took the initiative in 1936 in setting up the Population Investigation Committee, under the chairmanship of Professor (later Sir Alexander) Carr-Saunders, to develop systems of analysis and put forward such statistics as they could muster to try to predict what was happening[8]. By this time the Government also recognised that its methods of obtaining and keeping important vital statistics were unsatisfactory and incomplete. In

A P Herbert opposes the Population (Statistics) Bill (*Hansard*, 1938)

In 1937 was a rumour going round
That Income Tax was soon to be six shillings in the pound;
The cost of education every season seemed to swell;
And to everyone's astonishment the population fell.

They pulled down all the houses where the children used to crowd
And built expensive blocks of flats where children weren't allowed;
So if father got a job there wasn't anywhere to dwell,
And everybody wondered why the population fell.

Abroad, to show that everyone was passionate for peace,
All children under seven joined the army or police;
The babies studied musketry while mothers filled a shell—
And everybody wondered why the population fell.

The world, in short, which never was extravagantly sane,
Developed all the signs of inflammation of the brain;
The past was not encouraging, the future none could tell,
But the Minister still wondered why the population fell.

For example, it would no doubt be advantageous for the purposes of vital statistics that the English birth registers should be improved upon the lines adopted by those *countries more advanced* in this respect in their statistical methods. It is, therefore, a matter for careful consideration, whether it might not be advisable to extend the Statutory Schedules laid down in the Registration Acts so as to contain the ages of the parents, the date of their marriage, the number of children born, and other particulars.

The Registrar General in 1904 considers widening the scope of the births registration data
(*Sixty-seventh Report of the Registrar General, 1904*)

1938 it took a major step to improve its information base when it brought before Parliament the Population (Statistics) Bill. This provided for additional questions to be asked whenever a birth was registered (see Chapter 3). The Bill met with opposition from both sides of the House on the grounds of unnecessary prying into personal matters and it was modified in several ways before being passed. A P Herbert, Independent MP for Oxford University, regarded the Bill as irrelevant and treated the House to a set of verses which he wrote for the occasion[9].

The Act put a duty on the registrar to note confidential particulars not recorded in the register (these have already been described in Chapter 3). It was the first big change in the scope of vital registration since the original Acts of 1836 and was immensely important for the future of demographic statistics. In particular it greatly extended the range of relevant information on fertility and, for the first time, it became possible to compute age and marriage duration specific fertility rates, and to make estimates of the prospects for replacement. The changes were very much in line with the ideas put forward by William Farr in the 1860s and by the Registrar General, Sir William Dunbar, in his Annual Report for 1904. Similar proposals were outlined by Sir Bernard Mallet in his presidential address to the Royal Statistical Society in 1917.

The Royal Commission on Population

In 1937, shortly before the passing of the 1938 Population (Statistics) Act, the House of Commons had debated a motion to the effect that 'the tendency of the population to decline may well constitute a danger to the maintenance of the British Empire and the economic well-being of the nation, and requests His Majesty's government to institute an enquiry into and report on the problem, and its social and economic consequences and to make recommendations in regard thereto.' Many, however, were sceptical of the value of such an enquiry on the grounds that it was a well-known fact that the birth rate was below replacement level and, unless the enquiry's recommendations could be translated into effective action, it would be a waste of time and money. These discussions were still continuing when war broke out. The birth rate continued to fall and, in 1943, when thoughts began to turn to post-war reconstruction, a Royal Commission was set up under the chairmanship of, first, Sir John Simon and, after his resignation, Sir Hubert Henderson; W A B (later Sir Bryan) Hopkin was its assistant secretary. By the time the Commission reported in 1949, the birth rate was already increasing and it seemed highly unlikely that a decline in population was imminent.

Although few, if any, of the Commission's recommendations were adopted its range of enquiries and systematic approach had a profound influence on the development of demographic research. For example, part of the data collected consisted of a Family Census, taken in 1946, of 10 per cent of the female population. This was the largest enquiry of its kind since the Census of 1911 and it provided much new information on the pattern of fertility during the 1920s and 1930s: it was also the first occasion on which fertility was analysed on a cohort rather than a period basis. The enquiry was repeated in the 1971 Census. The Commission's Biological and Medical Committee also sponsored a survey by Dr Lewis Fanning into the practice of contraception, the first official enquiry into the subject.

The work undertaken on behalf of the Commission resulted in a better understanding of the demographic situation in Britain and, in the years which followed, less was heard about the supposed dysgenic effects of differential fertility. A further piece of evidence to allay any such fears resulted from collaboration between the Scottish Council for Research in Education and the Population Investigation Committee to find out whether a decline in measured intelligence had actually occurred. In 1947 a repeat survey was carried out in Scotland of 11 year-old schoolchildren to test whether intelligence had declined since the previous survey in 1932. The results showed that it had not.

The work of the Royal Commission also led to closer collaboration between academics and the official statisticians in the GRO. The Commission urged that the professional statistical staff in the GRO should be strengthened and that the Registrar General should also be a professional statistician rather than an administrator. In these early post-war years (as in the inter-war period), there were two chief statisticians under the Registrar General, one for medical and the other for general statistics, and there is little doubt that for the work which needed doing they were too few in number and at a disadvantage in relation to the administrators. The Census of Population, for example was becoming immensely more complex and the advent of the computer required detailed planning to be carried out well in advance of the census date. Had the advice of the professional statisticians been better heeded at the GRO in 1961, it is likely that many of the delays and mistakes which occurred in the 1961 Census might have been avoided[10].

It was not until 1972 (more than twenty years after the Royal Commission made its recommendation) that a professional statistician was appointed as Registrar General when George Payne succeeded Michael Reed. His appointment followed the reorganisation of the Government Statistical Service under Sir Claus Moser, who had become its head in 1967. This reorganisation, which has already been described in Chapter 4, was immensely important for the GRO. It led to the appointment of further chief statisticians and the upgrading of the status of the Registrar General himself to the rank of deputy secretary. When George ('Toby') Payne retired in 1978 he was succeeded by Roger Thatcher, also a professional statistician. In December 1986, this now greatly respected post has once more gone to an administrator from the Department of Health and Social Security. The new Registrar General, Mrs Theresa Banks, takes over in one of the highest ranks in the Civil Service and with a background well tuned to the statistical needs of the country.

The Population Panel and the rise in the birth rate

The rise in the birth rate between 1955 and 1965 once again attracted public interest to population problems. Fears of population decline gave way to preoccupation with the prospect of too fast a growth both in Britain and overseas. The government responded by appointing a Population Panel, at the end of 1971, 'to assess the available evidence about the significance of population growth for both public affairs and private life in this country at the present and in prospect'. The Panel, which reported at the end of 1972 and published its report early the next year, concluded that 'the situation was not such as to require immediate policy initiatives designed to reduce dramatically the rate of (population) increase', but it did stress the importance for government to take more account of the population situation when considering policy options. Developments in economic and social policies during the post-war years had resulted in much greater interest in population projections. For example, the Department of Health and Social

Security, the Department of Employment and the Department of Education and Science, as well as the local authorities and those responsible for regional planning, needed information on the future numbers, composition and structure of the population and its geographical distribution by age and marital status as a basis for their policies. The Population Panel thus stressed that there was an urgent need to improve knowledge of the causes and implications of population trends. It also recommended that facilities for academic work outside government should be strengthened: this led to the setting up of the Centre for Population Studies, a department of the University of London.

The fall in the birth rate, which continued uninterruptedly from 1966 until 1977, greatly reduced the sense of urgency. The problem, once again, seemed to be disappearing of its own accord and the prospect of having to cope with a population of 70 million by the end of the century, which had been put forward in some of the projections in the 1960s, was receding. Indeed the birth rate now is well below replacement level, and has been so since 1972.

Some facts and figures

These concluding paragraphs summarise some of the major changes which have taken place in the population of England and Wales in the 150 years of the existence of the GRO.

In 1837, when the young Queen Victoria came to the throne, there were about 15 million people in England and Wales. Today there are 50 million. Not only are there more people but they are concentrated in different parts of England and Wales and many more live in urban areas. At the beginning of the eighteenth century only about a quarter of the population lived in towns of more than 20,000 people whereas today the proportion is about three quarters. The old centres of manufacturing industry in Wales, the midlands and the north of England have declined and the newer service and technology industries have moved towards the south.

England and Wales now contain a far greater proportion of people born overseas. Today they account for some six per cent of the population and, of these, about half describe themselves as white. Many have come from the New Commonwealth countries and there is accordingly a wide variety of people from different ethnic backgrounds. Many have settled in Britain and nearly a half of the non-white population have been born here.

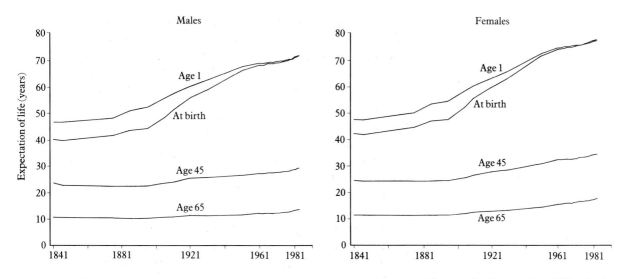

Chart 11.8   Expectation of life at birth and at selected ages, England and Wales, 1841–1984

One of the biggest changes has been in expectation of life. For males born in 1841 the expectation of life was 40 years and for females 42 years. Today the figures are 72 and 78 years respectively. At the beginning of the period many babies died during the first year of life, but once that first birthday had been reached expectation of life increased to 47 years for males and 48 years for females. Infant mortality remained high until the end of the century but thereafter fell steeply. Whereas in 1841 as many as one baby in six died before reaching the age of one year, today the proportion is one in a hundred. The marked difference between the life chances of those born into the higher social classes, however, has persisted and shows no signs of diminishing.

During the rest of childhood, infectious diseases were the chief scourge and were the main cause of death in the population as a whole. During the present century the main killers so far have been chronic diseases such as cancer and heart disease. Moreover, in a population where there are relatively fewer children and many more older people, the diseases which cause death are predominantly those which afflict the middle-aged and the elderly.

The increase in longevity has had many social and economic repercussions, but one of its major effects has been on family life and family living patterns. It means, for example, that whereas many children in the past lost one or both of their parents when they were still young and few knew their grandparents, many today know both sets of grandparents and some their great-grandparents as well.

Fertility declined sharply, particularly after the late 1870s, and birth rates are now below replacement level. One of the biggest contrasts between today and 1837 is the attitude towards fertility control, which is now accepted and practised throughout society. Families are accordingly much smaller and there is far less difference between social classes. Nearly two thirds of women who married in the middle of the last century had five or more liveborn children, whereas today nearly two thirds of those who married some twenty years ago (and have more or less completed their families) have only one or two.

More boys are born than girls but, whereas their death rates as babies used to be higher, there is now very little difference. The decline in infant mortality has thus been one of the main factors affecting the balance between the sexes between the ages of 15 and 45 when most people marry: in the middle of the last century the proportion was about 92 males for every 100 females; it is now 102.

The relationship between the sexes has changed dramatically and a woman today has an independent status which can enable her to live a life of her own in a way which would have been hard to imagine in 1837. A number of factors have been responsible, but some of the more important have been those which the GRO has charted, such as control over fertility and the decline in family size combined with the better conditions which have reduced infant mortality and led to better health of mothers.

Attitudes to marriage have changed and divorce now attracts less social stigma. Whereas in 1837 divorce required a private Act of Parliament, subsequent legislation beginning in 1857 has made civil divorce increasingly accessible without recourse to Parliament. If the current levels of divorce continue, one in three couples marrying today can expect to divorce. Many couples live together in stable unions outside marriage and many too, including single parents, bring up children without having married (Chart 11.9).

One of the most fundamental changes affecting attitudes to life has been the different age structure of the population. Chart 11.10 shows a broad pyramid shape for 1841, resulting from a combination of high fertility and high mortality rates. The much more rectangular shape in 1985 results from low fertility and low mortality. In 1841 half the population was under the age of 20: today it is 35. In 1841 there were five children for every person over 60 whereas now the numbers are about equal. In addition to its more immediate effect on family life, this change has had far reaching political and social repercussions.

The changing structure of the population combined with rising living standards has resulted in much smaller households. Today there are only some two and a half persons per household, or not much more than half the number in the middle of the last century. Not only are there fewer children and more old people,

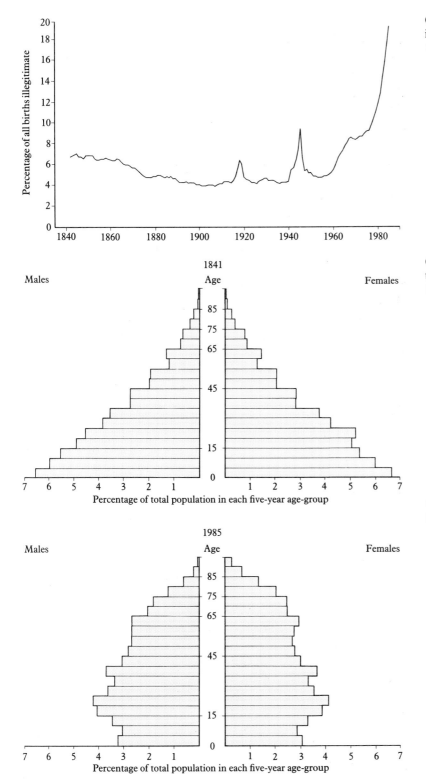

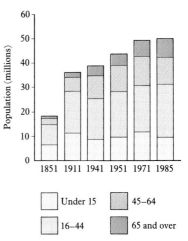

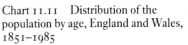

Chart 11.9   Percentage of all births illegitimate, England and Wales, 1838–1985

Chart 11.10   Sex and age structure of the population, England and Wales, 1841 and 1985

Chart 11.11   Distribution of the population by age, England and Wales, 1851–1985

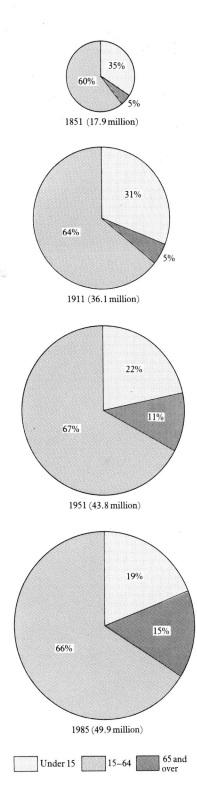

35%
60%
5%
1851 (17.9 million)

31%
64%
5%
1911 (36.1 million)

22%
67%
11%
1951 (43.8 million)

19%
66%
15%
1985 (49.9 million)

Under 15   15–64   65 and over

Chart 11.12   Age proportion of population of England and Wales, 1851, 1911, 1951 and 1985

but more young adults and more elderly people who can afford to live separately from their relatives.

A child born in 1837 would thus have opened its eyes on a very different world from one who is born in 1987. This history of births, marriages and deaths has charted some of the changes in the population and looked at some of the reasons why they have happened. Alice, before she followed the White Rabbit down the rabbit-hole, asked what is the use of a book without pictures or conversations; this book has told the 150 year history of the GRO with many illustrations and quotations from the past, and it is hoped that by so doing it has helped to bring the story to life.

References

1. David V Glass. *Numbering the People.* 1973, Farnborough, Saxon House.

2. E A Wrigley and R S Schofield. *The History of Population in England, 1551–1861.* 1981, London, Arnold.

3. E A Wrigley and R S Schofield. Op. cit.

4. J Matthews Duncan. *Fecundity, Fertility, Sterility and Allied Topics.* 1866, Edinburgh, Black.

5. Edwin Cannan. The probability of a cessation of the growth of population in England and Wales during the next century, in *The Economic Journal*, Vol. 5 No. 20, Dec. 1895.

6. E Grebenik. *Demographic Research in Britain, 1936–86.* Paper presented to the annual conference of the British Society of Population Studies on Population Research in Britain. 1986, University of East Anglia.

7. E Grebenik op. cit.

8. Enid Charles. *The Twilight of Parenthood.* 1934, London, Watts and Co.

9. D V Glass. Op. cit. Appendix 3, The Background of the Population (Statistics) Act of 1938.

10. Bernard Benjamin. A Statistician in the Public Health Service, in *The Making of Statisticians*, ed. J Gani. 1982, New York, Springer-Verlag.

Chronology of main events in the history of the Office

1538 **Parochial registers** introduced by Henry VIII.

1590 **National register** rejected as proposed by Elizabeth I's Lord Treasurer Lord Burghley.

1653 **Act** passed for civil marriage ceremony.

1735 **Bills of mortality** introduced.

1754 **Lord Hardwicke's Act** introduced stringent measures for marriage ceremonies.

1801 **Census of Population** – the first for Great Britain; carried out by Overseers of the Poor and local clergy in England and Wales and by schoolmasters in Scotland.

1811 **Census of Population**

1821 **Census of Population** – first to ask people their age.

1831 **Census of Population** – enumerators used tally counting method.

1833 **House of Commons Select Committee** recommended state registration of births, deaths and marriages.

1834 **Poor Law Act** established Board of Guardians.

1836 **Births and Deaths Registration Act and Marriage Act** established the Office of Registrar General; inaugurated the modern system of civil registration based on the Board of Guardians, which enabled statistics on the number of births, deaths and marriages to be produced.
First Registrar General appointed: Thomas Henry Lister.

1837 **General Register Office** for England and Wales established at Somerset House. Civil marriage ceremonies and system of civil registration of births, deaths and marriages introduced on 1 July.
Public Search Room established at Somerset House.

1839 **First classification of causes of death** devised by Dr William Farr, GRO and published in the first Annual Report of the Registrar General.

1840 **Registrar General's** *Weekly Returns* of deaths in the Metropolis introduced.

1841 **Census of Population** – first to be conducted by the Registrar General based on the system of civil registration in England and Wales; first in which householders completed their own forms; first to include individual names, country of birth and nationality questions.

1842 **Second Registrar General** appointed: George Graham.

1851 **Census of Population** – people first asked marital status and relationship to head of household.

1854 **Mid-year population estimates** for London first produced.

1855 **General Register Office (Scotland)** established with system of civil registration in Scotland.

1857 **First Matrimonial Causes Act** allowed civil divorce without the necessity of a private Act of Parliament.

1861 **Census of Population** – first to be carried out in Scotland as well as England and Wales based on registration service.

1864 **General Register Office (Ireland)** established.

1865 **Mid-year population estimates** for large towns.

1866   **Death indexes** first to record age at death.
1871   **Census of Population**
1872   **First Public Health Act**
1874   **Births and Deaths Registration Act** transferred the obligation to register births and deaths from the registrar to the person directly concerned; medical certification of cause of death was also required.
1880   **Third Registrar General** appointed: Sir Brydges Powell Hennicker.
1881   **Census of Population**
        Mid-year population estimates produced for *all* registration counties and large towns.
1888   **Local government boundaries** reformed.
1889   **Infectious diseases** – notification of certain diseases made compulsory in London.
1891   **Census of Population**
1898   **Marriage Act** created Authorised Persons for Nonconformist Places of Worship; enabled religious marriages to be solemnised in presence of Authorised Person instead of registrar.
1899   **Infectious diseases** – notification made compulsory in every urban, rural and port sanitary district in England and Wales.
1900   **Fourth Registrar General** appointed: Sir Reginald MacLeod.
1901   **Census of Population** – people first asked how many rooms they had.
        Infectious diseases – Registrar General's *Weekly Returns* expanded and extended to the administrative county of London and 32 large towns.
1902   **Fifth Registrar General** appointed: Sir William Cospatrick Dunbar.
1909   **Sixth Registrar General** appointed: Sir Bernard Mallet.
1911   **Census of Population** – the first to be partially processed by machine; fertility questions first asked.
        Mid-year population estimates produced for all local authority areas.
        Registrar General's social classes introduced as a means of analysing population statistics according to the general standing in the community of occupation/employment status groups.
        Birth indexes first contain maiden surname of mother.
        Second revision of International list of causes of deaths adopted by Medical Statistics Division.
1912   **Marriage indexes** first show surname of second party to marriage alongside name and surname of the other party.
1915   **National Registration Act** under the authority of Registrar General, provided for the compilation by local authorities of adult registers and the issue of 'certificates of registration'.
1919   **Ministry of Health** formed with a Minister for Health.
1920   **Census Act 1920** provided for taking of all future censuses by Registrars General, and for superintendent registrars and registrars and other persons to perform duties in connection with taking of censuses.
1921   **Census of Population** – asked questions about dependent children and orphans.
        Seventh Registrar General appointed: Sir Sylvanus P Vivian.
1922   **Registrar General's Weekly Return** included statistical returns of notifiable diseases.
1923   **Matrimonial Causes Act** allowed wives to petition for divorce on same basis as husbands.
1926   **First Adoption of Children Act** provided for adoption of infants; Adopted Children Register to be maintained by Registrar General.

Legitimacy Act provided for re-registration of illegitimate births if the parents marry each other.

Births and Deaths Registration Act 1926 required registrar's certificate or coroner's order before burial or cremation of body; medical certificate of death to be prescribed: still-births to be registered.

1927 **Still-births** first registered.

1928 **Private Member's Bill** introduced to change payment of registration officer to salaried basis.

1929 **Local Government Act** transferred functions of civil registration to local authorities with payment of registration officers on salaried basis.

Age of Marriage Act raised minimum age to 16 years.

1931 **Census of Population** – usual address question introduced.

1937 **Matrimonial Causes Act** extended the grounds for divorce to include desertion, cruelty and supervening incurable insanity.

1938 **Population (Statistics) Act** gave the Registrar General powers to collect certain information on a confidential basis at registration of births and deaths.

1939 **National Registration Act** provided for the establishment of national register of entire population; identity cards issued; Registrar General responsible for enumeration of population and maintenance of register and to issue identity cards.

1941 **Wartime Social Survey** formed, later became Social Survey Division of COI.

1945 **Eighth Registrar General** appointed: Sir George North.

1945–9 **Royal Commission on Population**

1946 **Family Census**

1947 **Short Birth Certificate** introduced.

1948 **Cancer registration** scheme introduced.

1949 **Marriage Act** consolidated measures for solemnisation and registration of marriages, with corrections and improvements.

Records of Births and Deaths in aircraft started for births and deaths occurring in any part of the world in any aircraft registered in Great Britain and Northern Ireland.

Royal Commission of Population reported.

1951 **Census of Population** – questions about household amenities (baths, WCs etc) introduced. Last census directly involving registrars.

Socio-economic groups introduced as a means of analysis based on similarity of social and economic status.

1952 **National Health Service Central Register** formed from National Registration records.

1953 **Registration Service Act** consolidated measures for registration service in England and Wales.

Births and Deaths Registration Act consolidated measures for registration of births and deaths in England and Wales.

Hospital In-patient Enquiry first carried out.

1957 **Family Expenditure Survey** started on behalf of the Department of Employment.

1958 **Ninth Registrar General** appointed: Edward Michael T Firth.

1960 **Population (Statistics) Act** made permanent Population (Statistics) Act 1938 and modified the confidential items collected at birth registration.

1961   **Census of Population** – the first to be processed by computer; some Small Area Statistics first published.
International Passenger Survey begun.
Still-birth weight statistics first collected.

1963   **Tenth Registrar General** appointed: Michael Reed.

1964   **International Passenger Survey** first used for collecting international migration statistics.
Congenital malformations first reported on a national basis.

1966   **Sample Census** – questions on car availability and means of transport to work introduced.

1968   **Legal abortion statistics** first collected.
Regional population projections begun, to assist with regional planning.

1969   **Family Law Reform Act** age of majority reduced from 21 to 18, provided for re-registration of births of illegitimate children to include particulars of the father in the register.
Death indexes first show deceased's date of birth.
Divorce Reform Act replaced the concept of guilty and innocent partner by sole criterion of irretrievable breakdown of marriage.

1970   General Register Office and Government Social Survey combined to form the **Office of Population Censuses and Surveys** – OPCS.
General Household Survey begun sponsored by Central Statistical Office.
Marriage (Registrar General's Licence) Act permitted marriage in special circumstances.

1971   **Census of Population**
Internal migration statistics produced using National Health Service Central Register.

1972   **Eleventh Registrar General** appointed: George Paine.
Public Search Room and OPCS started move to St Catherines House.

1973   **Population Panel** report published.
Labour Force Survey started on biennial basis as part of statistical obligation to European Community.
Longitudinal Study set up.

1975   **Live birth weight** information collected.
Population Trends official journal of OPCS first issued.
OPCS **annual review volumes** by subject matter introduced.
Children Act 1975 provided for adult adopted people to be given information on birth entry.

1978   **Twelfth Registrar General** appointed: Roger Thatcher.

1981   **Census of Population**
Industrial Diseases (Notification) Act provided for certification of deaths and recording of information relating to industrial diseases.

1983   **Marriage Act 1983** enabled marriage ceremony at residence of house-bound or detained person.

1983   **Labour Force Survey** expanded to become annual and continuous.

1984   **Matrimonial and Family Proceedings Act** allowed divorce to be petitioned after the first anniversary of marriage.

1985   **Marriage (Prohibited Degrees of Relationship) Act** allowed persons related to one another by affinity to marry, in certain restricted circumstances.

1986   **Thirteenth Registrar General** appointed: Mrs Gillian Theresa Banks.

Registrars General 1837 – 1987   Appendix B

Thomas Henry Lister (Registrar General 1836–42) was born in 1801. He was appointed in 1836 as the first Registrar General and supervised the establishment of the General Register Office and the registration service. He also attained considerable literary celebrity as a novelist. He died in June 1842.

George Graham (Registrar General 1842–79) was born in 1801. He entered the East India Company Service and retired as a Major in 1831 having been Military Secretary in Bombay between 1828 and 1830. He became Private Secretary to his brother Sir James Graham on his appointment as Secretary of State for the Home Department in Peel's Ministry in 1841. He died in May 1888 aged 86.

Sir Brydges Hennicker (Registrar General 1880–1900) was born in 1835 and educated at Eton. He served in the army with the 68th Foot and then the Royal Horse Guards until his retirement in 1859. He died in 1906.

Sir Reginald McLeod (Registrar General 1900–02) was born on the Isle of Skye in 1847 and educated at Harrow and Trinity College, Cambridge. Between 1889 and 1900 he served as Queen's and Lord Treasurer's Remembrancer being appointed Registrar General in 1900. In 1902 he became Under Secretary for Scotland. He died in August 1935.

Sir William Cospatrick Dunbar (Registrar General 1902–09) was born in 1904. He served in the Home Office between 1868 and 1885 acting as Private Secretary to successive Under Secretaries of State in the period 1875 to 1885. Until 1902 he served as Assistant Under Secretary for Scotland. He died in February 1931.

Sir Bernard Mallet (Registrar General 1909–20) was born in 1859 and was educated at Clifton College and Balliol College, Oxford. He joined the Foreign Office in 1882 moving to the Treasury in 1885 where he was Private Secretary to the Parliamentary Secretary to the Treasury. He was also Private Secretary to the First Lord between 1891 and 1892, and again from 1895 to 1897. Before becoming Registrar General in 1909 he was Commissioner of Inland Revenue. He died in October 1932.

Sir Sylvanus Vivian (Registrar General 1921–45) was born on 1 October 1880 and was educated at St Paul's School and St John's College, Oxford. In 1903 he entered the Inland Revenue and subsequently served in the Ministries of Food and of National Service before becoming Registrar General in 1921. He died in 1958.

Sir George North (Registrar General 1945–58) was born on 23 March 1895 and was educated at St Andrews College and Trinity College, Dublin. After the First World War he was called to the Bar of Lincoln's Inn but in 1921 he joined the Home Civil Service and was appointed to the Ministry of Health. He died in 1971.

Edward Michael Tyndall Firth (Registrar General 1958–63) was born in 1903 and educated at King Edward VII School, Sheffield and University College, Oxford. He joined the Inland Revenue in 1926 and moved to the Ministry of Health in 1945.

Michael Reed (Registrar General 1963–72) was born in 1912 and educated at Christ's Hospital and Jesus College, Cambridge. He joined the Ministry of Health in 1935 working at one time as Private Secretary to the Minister of Health. From 1958 he served in the Cabinet Office returning to the Ministry of Health in 1961. He was appointed Registrar General in 1963 and became the first Director of the Office of Population Censuses and Surveys in 1971. He died in December 1985.

George Paine (Registrar General 1972–78) was born in 1918 and educated at Bradfield College and Peterhouse, Cambridge. In 1941 he joined the Ordnance Board and after service in the RAF, the Ministry of Agriculture in 1948. He subsequently worked at the Inland Revenue, the Central Statistical Office and the Board of Trade before becoming, in 1957, Director of Statistics and Intelligence at the Board of Inland Revenue.

Roger Thatcher (Registrar General 1978–86) was born in Birmingham in 1926 and attended the Leys School, Cambridge and then St John's College before national service in the Royal Navy. He began his career in the civil service in 1952 when he joined the Admiralty as a Statistician. After two years in the Cabinet Office he joined the Ministry of Labour in 1963 as Chief Statistician becoming Director of Statistics in the Department of Employment.

Gillian Theresa Banks (Registrar General 1986–   ) was born in 1933 and went to Lady Margaret Hall, Oxford. She joined the Colonial Office in 1955 and went to India with her husband in 1960. On return she joined the Treasury, and in 1972 transferred to the Department of Health and Social Security to work on health service finance and planning. When the NHS Management Board was established in 1985 she was appointed Director of Health Authority Finance.

Some recent OPCS publications

Appendix C

Reference series

Abortion statistics (Series AB)

Abortion statistics 1985 England and Wales. Series AB no. 12 (1986). ISBN 0 11 691073 9 (£6.20)

Mortality statistics (Series DH)

Mortality statistics 1985. Series DH1 no. 17 (1987). ISBN 0 11 691189 1 (£5.20)

Mortality statistics: cause 1985. Series DH2 no. 12 (1987). ISBN 0 11 691198 0 (£6.80)

Mortality statistics: perinatal and infant (social and biological factors) 1985. Series DH3 no. 18 (1987). ISBN 0 11 691194 8 (£5.80)

Mortality statistics: childhood 1985. Series DH3 no. 19 (1987). ISBN 0 11 691198 0 (£6.80)

Mortality statistics: accidents and violence 1985. Series DH4 no. 11 (1987). ISBN 0 11 691195 6 (£5.20)

Mortality statistics: area 1985 (microfiche). Series DH5 no. 12 (1987). ISBN 0 11 691180 8 (£8.90 net)

Demographic Review (Series DR)

Demographic review, 1987, Great Britain: Series DR no. 2 (in preparation).

Decennial Supplements (Series DS)

Occupational mortality 1979–80, 1982–83, Great Britain. Series DS no. 6 (1986)
    Part 1 Commentary   ISBN 0 11 691174 3 (£9.20)
    Part 2 Microfiche   ISBN 0 11 691175 1 (£40.00 plus VAT)
English Life Tables no. 14, 1980–1982 England and Wales. Series DS no. 7 (1987). ISBN 0 11 691067 4 (£4.10)

Electoral statistics (Series EL)

Electoral statistics 1987 England and Wales, Scotland and Northern Ireland. Series EL no. 14 (1987). ISBN 0 11 691196 4 (£4.10)

Family statistics (Series FM)

Birth statistics 1985. Series FM1 no. 12 (1986). ISBN 0 11 691072 0 (£8.00)

Birth statistics: historical series 1837–1983. Series FM1 no. 13 (1987). ISBN 0 11 691187 5 (£10.70)

Period and cohort birth order statistics (microfiche). Series FM1 no. 14 (1987). ISBN 0 11 691189 3 (£7.50 net)

Marriage and divorce statistics 1984. Series FM2 no. 11 (1986). ISBN 0 11 690757 6 (£8.00)

Longitudinal study (Series LS)

Longitudinal study: social class and occupational mobility, 1971–1977. Series LS no. 2
   (1985). ISBN 0 11 691134 4 (£7.40)

Morbidity statistics (Series MB)

Cancer statistics: registrations 1983. Series MB1 no. 15 (1986). ISBN
   0 11 691184 0 (£8.00)
Communicable disease statistics 1985. Series MB2 no. 12 (1987). ISBN
   0 11 691199 9 (£6.20)
Congenital malformation statistics: notifications 1971–80. Series MB3 no. 1 (1983).
   ISBN 0 11 690979 X (£7.40)
Hospital In-patient Enquiry summary tables 1985. Series MB4 no. 26 (1987). ISBN
   0 11 691201 4 (£6.20)
Hospital In-patient Enquiry main tables (microfiche) 1984. Series MB4 no. 25 (1987).
   ISBN 0 11 690771 1 (£10.00)
Morbidity statistics from general practice 1981–82 (microfiche). Series MB5 no. 1
   (1986). ISBN 0 11 690756 8 (£15.90 net)

International migration (Series MN)

International migration 1984 United Kingdom, England and Wales. Series MN no. 11
   (1986). ISBN 0 11 691162 X (£5.20)

Population estimates and projections (Series PP and VS)

Population projections 1983–2023 (microfiche). Series PP2 no. 13 (1985). ISBN
   0 11 691145 X (£8.20 plus VAT)
Variant population projections 1983–2023 (microfiche). Series PP2 no. 14 (1986).
   ISBN 0 11 690777 0 (£7.30 net)
Population projections area England 1983–2001. Series PP3 no. 6 (1986). ISBN
   0 11 691178 6 (£5.20)
Population and vital statistics; local and health authority area summary 1985. Series
   VS/PP1 no. 12/8 (1987). ISBN 0 11 691186 7 (£7.40)

Social Survey reports

General Household Survey, 1984. Series SS 457M (1986). ISBN 0 11 691185 9
   (£11.70)
The West Indian School Leaver, by Ken Sillitoe and Howard Meltzer. Series SS no.
   465 (1986).
   Vol 1 Starting work ISBN 0 11 691150 6 (£13.95)
   Vol 2 The next five years ISBN 0 11 691153 0 (£13.95)
Labour Force Survey 1983 and 1984. Series LFS no. 4 (1986). ISBN
   0 11 691129 8 (£6.80)
Who would prefer separate accommodation? by Irene Rauta. Series SS 1125. ISBN
   0 11 691163 8 (£13.00)
1981 Census post-enumeration survey, by Malcolm Britton and Francis Birch. Series
   SS 1158 (1985). ISBN 0 11 691139 5 (£15.50)
Differences in drinking patterns between selected regions, by Elizabeth Breeze. Series
   SS 1161 (1985). ISBN 0 11 691115 8 (£12.00)
Staff attitudes to the prison service, by Alan Marsh, Joy Dobbs, Janet Monk and
   Amanda White. Series SS 1175 (1985). ISBN 0 11 691127 1 (£13.00)
Family planning in Scotland, by Margaret Bone. Series SS 1177 (1985). ISBN
   0 11 691147 6 (£10.50)

Changing the definition of a household, by Jean Todd and David Griffiths. Series SS 1182 (1986). ISBN 0 11 681071 2 (£8.50)

Women and drinking, by Elizabeth Breeze. Series SS 1185 (1985). ISBN 0 11 691146 8 (£14.10)

Children's dental health in the United Kingdom 1983, by Jean E Todd and Tricia Dodd. Series SS 1189 (1985). ISBN 0 11 691136 0 (£13.00)

Recent private lettings 1982–84, by Jean E Todd. Series SS 1212(A) (1986). ISBN 0 11 691066 6 (£5.80)

Smoking among secondary school children in 1984, by Joy Dobbs and Alan Marsh. Series SS 1215 (1985). ISBN 0 11 691149 2 (£10.50)

Drinking and attitudes to licencing in Scotland, by Eileen Goddard. Series SS 1223 (1986). ISBN 0 11 691164 6 (£9.00)

Visiting the National Maritime Museum, by Malcolm Smyth and Barbara Ayton. Series SS 1226 (1985). ISBN 0 11 691152 2 (£7.60)

Adolescent drinking, by Alan Marsh, Joy Dobbs and Amanda White. Series SS 1209 (1986). ISBN 0 11 691182 4 (£6.80)

Young people's intentions to enter higher education, by Bob Redpath and Barbara Harvey. Series SS1231 (1987). ISBN 0 11 691200 6 (C £11.50)

Visiting the National Portrait Gallery, by Barbara Harvey. Series SS 1237 (1987). ISBN 0 11 691179 4 (£8.00)

1981 Census reports

The main series of 1981 Census publications include a national report on each of the following subjects: communal establishments; country of birth; economic activity; historical tables (1801–1981); household and family composition; housing and households; national migration; national report for Great Britain; persons of pensionable age; qualified manpower; sex, age, and marital status; usual residence; workplace and transport to work[1].

Other reports in the 1981 Census series of publications include:

Classification of occupations 1980. (1980) ISBN 0 11 690728 2 (£13.00)

Preliminary report, England and Wales. Series CEN 81 PR(1) (1981). ISBN 0 11 690755 X (£4.80)

Preliminary report for towns: urban and rural population, England and Wales. Series CEN 81 PR(2) (1982). ISBN 0 11 690923 4 (£4.80)

Index of place names, England and Wales. Two vols. A–K and L–Z. Series CEN 81 1PN (1985). ISBN 0 11 691065 8 (£35.00)

Key statistics for local authorities. Series CEN 81 KSLA(1983). ISBN 0 11 690980 3 (£9.10)

Key statistics for urban areas, Great Britain. Series CEN 81 KSUA 1(1984). ISBN 0 11 691064 X (£9.10)

Key statistics for urban areas, regional reports, England and Wales. Separate reports are available for the North, Midlands, South East, and South West and Wales. Series CEN 81 KSUA 2 to 5[1]

Regional migration reports, England and Wales (parts 1 and 2). Separate reports are available for East Anglia, East Midlands, North, North West, South East, South West, Yorkshire and Humberside, West Midlands and Wales. Series CEN 81 RM1 and RM1(2) to CEN 81 RM9 and RM9(2)[1]

County reports, England and Wales. Two reports are available for each county.

1. Full details of these publications are given in *Sectional List No. 56* (see Notes on page 153).

Report for Wales. Series CEN 81RW (1983). ISBN 0 11 690938 2 (£9.10). Welsh language version: Series CEN 81 AG (1984). ISBN 0 11 690939 0 (£9.10)

Welsh language in Wales. Series CEN 81WL (1983). ISBN 0 11 690941 2 (£5.00). Welsh language version: Series CEN 81 IG (1983). ISBN 0 11 690942 0 (£5.00)

People in Britain wallcharts (£2.00 each):

1. Population
2. Pensioners
3. London
4. Housing
5. Travel to work
6. Workforce

Census guides

1. *Britain's elderly population*. ISBN 0 904952 15 0 (£1.50)
2. *Britain's children*. ISBN 0 904952 22 3 (£1.50)
3. *Britain's workforce*. ISBN 0 904952 23 1 (£3.00)
4. *Britain's households*. ISBN 0 904952 27 4 (£3.00)

County Monitors. Series CEN 81 CM (1981) (Prices on application)

Parliamentary constituency Monitors. Series CEN 81 PCM (1982) (Prices on application)

Ward and civil parish Monitors. Series CEN 81 WCP (1983) (Prices on application)

Studies on medical and population subjects

Immigrant mortality in England and Wales 1970–78: cause of death by country of birth, by MG Marmot, AM Adelstein and L Bulusu. Series SMPS no. 47 (1984). ISBN 0 11 691094 1 (£13.00)

Socio-economic classification of local and health authorities of Great Britain, by John Craig. Series SMPS no. 48 (1985). ISBN 0 11 691138 7 (£8.20)

Infectious diseases during pregnancy, by PEM Fine, JA Clarkson, J Snowman, AM Adelstein and SM Evans. Series SMPS no. 49 (1985). ISBN 0 11 691143 3 (£6.20)

Occupational reproductive epidemiology, by ME McDowall. Series SMPS no. 50 (1985). ISBN 0 11 691141 7 (£8.90)

Cancer incidence and mortality in the vicinity of nuclear installations England and Wales 1959–80, by P Cook-Mozaffari, FL Ashwood, T Vincent, D Forman, M Alderson. Series SMPS no. 51 (1987). ISBN 0 11 691068 2 (£27.00)

Population Trends

Population Trends is the OPCS house journal. It is published quarterly, in March, June, September and December each year. In addition to bringing together articles on a variety of population and medical subjects it contains regular tables on: population, components of population change, vital statistics, live births, marriages, divorces, migration, deaths and abortions. (£5.00 per issue).

Occasional Papers

Statistical summaries of between-area differences for some 1981 Census variables, by John Craig. Occasional Paper no. 32 (1985). ISBN 0 904952 16 9 (£3.00)

William Farr 1807–1883 Commemorative symposium. Occasional Paper no. 33
(1985). ISBN 0 904952 17 7 (£3.00)

Measuring socio-economic change – Papers for BSPS Conference 9–11 September 1985.
Occasional Paper no. 34 (1985). ISBN 0 904952 20 7 (£4.50)

*A comparison of migration data from the National Health Service Central Register and
the 1981 Census,* by Tim Devis and Ian Mills. Occasional Paper no. 35 (1986).
ISBN 0 904952 24 X (£4.50).

Miscellaneous publications

Birth counts: statistics of pregnancy, by Alison MacFarlane and Miranda Mugford.
Vol. 1 Commentary (1984). ISBN 0 11 690965 X (£9.95). *Vol. 2 Tables* (1984).
ISBN 0 11 691084 4 (£19.95)

Notes

1. Full details of OPCS publications currently in print can be found in the HMSO
   catalogue *Government Publications Sectional List No. 56. Office of Population
   Censuses and Surveys,* available from the Publicity Department at HMSO (see
   address below).

2. Most of OPCS's reports are published by HMSO and are available from the HMSO
   Publications Centre (see address below), HMSO bookshops, accredited agents
   and good booksellers.

3. Census guides, census wall charts and OPCS Monitors are published by OPCS
   and are available from Information Branch, OPCS (see address below).

4. Addresses:

Information Branch   HMSO Publications Centre
OPCS   (Mail and telephone orders only)
St Catherines House   PO Box 276
10 Kingsway   London SW8 5DT
London WC2B 6JP   Telephone orders (01) 622 3316
                                      General enquiries (01) 211 5656

                                      HMSO Publicity Department
                                      St Crispins House
                                      Duke Street
                                      Norwich NR3 1PD

Appendix D   Historical tables

Table 1   Live births, still births, deaths, marriages and divorces; England and Wales, 1841–1985

Year	Live births			Stillbirths per 1,000 live and still births	Deaths		Marriages		Divorces per 1,000 married persons
	Crude birth rate (births per 1,000 population all ages)	General fertility rate (births per 1,000 women aged 15–44)	Illegitimate births per 1,000 total and live births		Crude death rate (deaths per 1,000 population all ages)	Infant death rate (deaths at age under 1 year per 1,000 live births)	Crude marriage rate (marriages per 1,000 population all ages)	Median age at marriage for spinsters	
1841	32.2	134	..	..	21.6	..	..	..	..
1851	34.2	145	68.2	..	22.0	154	..	23.38	..
1861	34.6	147	63.4	..	21.6	153	16.3	23.26	..
1871	35.0	152	56.1	..	22.6	158	16.7	23.07	..
1881	33.9	147	48.8	..	18.9	130	15.1	23.21	..
1891	31.4	132	42.4	..	20.2	149	15.6	23.66	..
1901	28.5	114	38.9	..	16.9	151	15.9	24.02	..
1911	24.4	98	42.7	..	14.6	130	15.2	24.47	..
1921	22.4	90	45.5	..	12.1	83	16.9	24.19	..
1931	15.8	64	44.4	40.9	12.3	65.7	15.6	24.21	..
1941	13.9	58	53.6	34.8	12.8	60.0	18.6	22.84	..
1951	15.5	72	48.4	23.0	12.5	29.7	16.5	22.60	2.6
1961	17.6	89	59.8	19.0	11.9	21.4	15.0	21.57	2.1
1971	15.9	83	83.9	12.5	11.5	17.5	16.5	21.40	5.9
1981	12.8	61	127.6	6.6	11.6	10.9	14.2	21.95	11.9
1982	12.6	60	143.6	6.3	11.7	10.6	13.8	22.12	12.1
1983	12.7	60	157.7	5.7	11.7	10.0	13.9	22.33	12.2
1984	12.8	60	173.5	5.7	11.4	9.3	14.0	22.58	12.0
1985	13.1	61	192.3	5.5	11.8	9.2	13.9	22.80	13.4

Table 2   Population, sex ratios and household size; England and Wales, 1841–1985

Year	Population (millions) in age-groups:					Sex ratio males per thousand females at ages:		Persons per household
	All ages	Under 15	15–44	45–64	65 and over	15–44	65 and over	
1841	15.9	5.4	6.9	2.0	0.7	93	85	..
1851	17.9	6.4	8.2	2.5	0.8	94	83	4.8
1861	20.1	7.2	9.1	2.9	0.9	92	83	4.5
1871	22.7	8.2	10.1	3.3	1.1	93	84	4.5
1881	26.0	9.5	11.6	3.7	1.2	94	82	4.6
1891	29.0	10.2	13.3	4.2	1.4	93	79	4.7
1901	32.5	10.5	15.6	4.8	1.5	92	77	4.6
1911	36.1	11.1	17.3	5.8	1.9	93	76	4.4
1921	37.9	10.5	17.8	7.3	2.3	88	75	4.1
1931	40.0	9.5	18.8	8.7	3.0	91	75	3.7
1951	43.8	9.7	18.7	10.6	4.9	97	69	3.2
1961	46.1	10.6	18.2	11.8	5.5	100	62	3.2
1971	48.7	11.6	18.8	11.8	6.5	102	62	2.9
1981	49.2	10.1	20.7	11.0	7.5	102	65	2.8
1982	49.6	9.9	21.1	11.0	7.6	102	65	..
1983	49.7	9.7	21.3	11.1	7.5	102	65	..
1984	49.8	9.6	21.6	11.2	7.5	102	65	..
1985	49.9	9.5	21.8	11.0	7.6	102	65	..

Data for 1841–1981 are taken from census reports; there was no census in 1941.

Index

Printed in the United Kingdom for Her Majesty's Stationery Office
Dd 240451 6/87, C45, 48739